FROM THE CONGO
TO CAPITOL HILL

FROM THE CONGO
TO CAPITOL HILL

A COMING-OF-AGE MEMOIR

STEPHEN R. WEISSMAN

Unconventional History Press

Washington, D.C.

From the Congo to Capitol Hill: A Coming-of-Age Memoir

Copyright © 2023 by Stephen R. Weissman. All Rights Reserved.

Publisher: Unconventional History Press, Washington, D.C.

For information about this title or to order other books and/or electronic media, contact the author: www.stephenrweissman.com

ISBNs:
979-8-9883321-0-7 (softcover)
979-8-9883321-1-4 (eBook)

Printed in the United States of America

Cover and Interior design: 1106 Design

Library of Congress Control Number: 2023912767

Cover: Photo by U.S. House of Representatives' Committee on Foreign Affairs, June 1989, of author greeting Zaire President Mobutu Sese Seko at a Committee tea. Author's Africa Subcommittee staff colleague, Adwoa Dunn-Mouton, looks on.

CONTENTS

PREFACE

❧

W*hy have I decided to write* about two long-ago engagements with the Democratic Republic of the Congo, as a professor at the Université Libre du Congo (ULC) in Kisangani (1969–71) and then a principal staff member of the U.S. House of Representatives Subcommittee on Africa (1979–91)? And why should anyone care?

In the first place, these were exceptionally interesting experiences that illuminate the history of post-colonial Africa and the post-Vietnam War U.S. Congress. Even more importantly, they provide insights into such burning contemporary issues as the dynamics of racial conflict, the paranoia and narcissism of authoritarian regimes, and the continuing dysfunctions of Congress, the State Department, and portions of the American press. Because I was not only a witness to these events but also a direct participant in them, I'm able to provide readers with an unusually full account.

In addition, I believe that many people, regardless of whether they are interested in Africa, Congress, or foreign policy, could benefit from the more personal aspects of my tale. The risky, sometimes mistaken, choices that I made in the Congo and Congress put me on a tortuous—sometimes humorous—path toward personal growth and political maturity. There are, I think, some helpful cautions here for anyone who calculates whether to take a risk in their professional life or seeks to become a more effective change-agent within democratic institutions.

Although I use the memoir form, that does not mean that my book is based mainly upon my recollections. The memories are there, but they build upon and are corroborated by considerable independent evidence.

Since I was never a member of the executive branch of the American government, many of the relevant records cannot be easily located in public archives. Nevertheless, I possess ample documentation.

Part I is largely constructed from materials I gathered during my time at the ULC and afterward: student newsletters, official publications and communiques, faculty meeting minutes, local newspaper stories, dozens of letters my wife Nancy and I wrote to our relatives during our fifteen months in Kisangani, Nancy's own journal, and my subsequent communications with former colleagues and students.

Part II draws significantly from my personal files from twelve years as a congressional subcommittee staff aide, which include internal subcommittee memoranda, briefing materials, reports, notes, and correspondence. In a few places, I refer to interviews I later conducted with members of Congress.

Especially, but not only, in Part II, I have also tapped into various publicly available sources such as Congressional hearings, scholarly studies, declassified U.S. government documents, and stories from American and foreign media. These sources are cited in endnotes.

Preface

Please note that the post-Independence Congo Republic (also known as Congo-Kinshasa) was renamed Zaire in 1971. It adopted its current appellation, Democratic Republic of the Congo, in 1997.

~~~

PART I

A Bend in the River:
Kisangani

CHAPTER 1

A FORCED DEPARTURE

~~~

It was a cloudy, humid, altogether uninspiring Saturday morning in the fabled town jutting out of Africa's equatorial rain forest. The city's new name, Kisangani—Swahili for "The City on the Island"—reflected its location at the confluence of the Congo River and several tributaries. Foreigners knew it better by its Belgian colonial designation, Stanleyville. It had been christened by King Leopold II in honor of Henry Morton Stanley, the American journalist he hired as his "Chief of Expedition" who established the trading station on the Congo River in 1883. Over the next century, it would become the unnamed setting for two of the most influential works of fiction on Africa: Joseph Conrad's *Heart of Darkness* and V.S. Naipaul's *A Bend in the River*. These books traced the arc of Congo's modern political history: from the horror-filled beginning of Belgian colonization to the reign of the Congolese "Big Man"—President Mobutu Sese Seko.

On this 27th day of March 1971, I was about to be publicly fired by a government vice-minister from my job as associate professor of political science at the Université Libre du Congo (ULC) and ordered to fly, with my wife Nancy and

3

our three-year-old son Daniel, to the capital the same afternoon and "report" to the country's chief cop. Such was the
dramatic conclusion of my first engagement with the Congo,
one in which I personally experienced the volatility of racial
conflict, the paranoia of an authoritarian regime, and the
consequences of my failure to fully anticipate the costs of my
words and actions.

The Protestant-sponsored ULC was 80 percent funded by
the Congo government, but its operations had been largely
led by U.S. Protestant missionaries. I was one of seventeen
Americans within a mainly European teaching corps of 100.
Having recently obtained my Ph.D. in political science from
the University of Chicago with a dissertation on *American
Foreign Policy in the Congo 1960–1964*, I was fulfilling my
dream of inhabiting the country I had been studying and
writing about for four years. I had left behind all my routines,
friends, and relatives. Although I was living under a kind of
political dictatorship, I had never felt so free.

The academic community had been summoned to a 9:00
a.m. meeting in front of the white, bow-shaped administrative
building to learn the university administration's response to
its latest crisis. This time the blow-up had been big enough for
the president to dispatch two vice-ministers to the campus.

For weeks, the 116 members of the sophomore class of my
economics and social sciences faculty—15 percent of the student body—had been boycotting a Dutch professor's "Political
Economy" course, alleging that he was incompetent to teach
it. All efforts by the university administration to resolve the
conflict had failed. Lately, some of the students had gone so
far as to insult the university's brand new Congolese acting

rector. One student reportedly spit on him, and others had disrupted his office. They had also vandalized the faculty dean's car, deflating its tires and removing its battery. Finally, the university had expelled seventy boycotters for refusing an ultimatum to return to class. However, the students were given to understand that they could be reinstated if they went to the provincial governor's office and apologized. But when they showed up, they were arrested and held overnight at Kisangani's main public high school. A newly arrived American professor who attempted to take pictures of their "apology" was beaten by the police and imprisoned for hours. There were rumors of an imminent strike by the entire student body.

As I joined dozens of faculty members and hundreds of students milling around the dusty road in front of the administration building, I spotted Alistair Weir in his customary short-sleeved white shirt and brown shorts, chatting with his dean. Alistair, a Scot, and his American wife Mary taught theology and were Nancy's and my closest friends in Kisangani. They believed that foreign missionaries like themselves should be helping the Congolese Church "decolonize"—become more authentically "national" in character. In their polite but persistent quest, they were gentle thorns in the side of the older, more conservative Dutch dean of theology. Seeing me approach, Alistair quickly moved to my side. Nodding in the direction of his dean, he whispered, "He says you're going to be fired!"

I stood there, stunned. How could this be? I had been teaching a political science course to the boycotting sophomores but had stood apart from their protest. The only thing I'd done was to ask a couple of students I had encountered while picking up my mail what was happening. Knowing first-hand the students' yearning for good teaching, I suspected they had legitimate grounds for complaint. But I lacked objective information about either the quality of Professor "G's" class or the nature of the "compromises" the students had reportedly spurned. Having been scarred by earlier tangles arising from my sympathy for Congolese student and faculty grievances against the previous conservative White missionary-led administration, I was anxious to avoid trouble during the last four months of my teaching contract. Maybe, I hoped, Alistair's dean was just repeating a rumor that one of my critics had floated.

As I waited nervously—this young, auburn-haired, bespectacled American in a colorful East African "bubu" shirt and blue jeans—two men in Western suits and ties emerged from the crowd in front of me. They were the vice-ministers of the Interior and Education. The former presented their decisions for the university. All the sophomore class boycotters were forthwith expelled. Seven student "ringleaders" were under arrest and would depart immediately for Kinshasa. After each of these pronouncements the students, standing together to the left of the vice-ministers, emitted a disapproving grunt. There was a long pause. Perhaps, I ruminated, the unhappy show was over. Suddenly the vice-minister called out my name and commanded me to step forward.

As I somewhat sheepishly came before him, he snapped, *"Ôtez les mains des poches!"* (Take your hands out of your pockets!) Withdrawing my hands, I felt like an errant child about to be punished. The thought occurred to me, "Was this how he felt growing up under Belgian colonialism? Did some Belgian teacher or official ever use the same expression with him?" Then came the dreaded condemnation: "Professor Weissman," he commanded, "I want you out of the university. You, your wife, and child must fly to Kinshasa today and report directly to the minister of the interior." A few seconds passed. The students emitted their third, loud dissenting grunt and the meeting concluded. A subsequent university communiqué relayed the government's determination that any student or professor "recognized to have played the role of leader, directly or indirectly, would be expelled and if necessary, brought to justice."

Shell-shocked as I was, my first impulse was to seek some rational explanation for what I had just heard. I knew the vice-ministers had parachuted into the tense situation only the day before and had spent much of their time conversing with top university officials. So I crossed the dirt road to a section of grass where the latter had gathered. They were willing to chat with me, but some of what they said sounded like buck-passing.

With an air of cool detachment, the slight, bespectacled acting rector, Jean-Felix Koli, bearing a leopard-skin cap and grasping a walking stick just like those of President Mobutu, remarked, "You know, the president has an intelligence office at the university." But if this was about a secret agency's paranoia about some role I was playing in the boycott, I thought university officials might have inquired about what evidence they had. After all, Koli was not just a university bureaucrat but a member of Parliament from the president's home region who might be able to influence the government. (On the other hand, he was an ambitious politician anxious not to displease his patron.) Then I turned to "A," the tall, genial Dutch vice-rector for academic affairs who represented the university's partnership with the Protestant-founded Free University of Amsterdam. But he too cast responsibility elsewhere. It was the Congolese administrators' decision to accuse me, he confided, with a look of post-colonial helplessness.

Neither Koli nor A mentioned any specific allegations against me. Those I finally obtained from Edouard Sendwe, the U.S.-educated Congolese vice-rector for student affairs. "The main charge against you," he explained, "was your course on Mao and your distribution of Maoist tracts to the students." He casually added, "You shouldn't have been seen with the students."

By now, my mental state had dissolved into a crazy stew of anxiety, indignation, and a sense of absurdity bordering on hilariousness. I wasn't giving a course on Mao Zedong, I protested to Sendwe and the others standing nearby, but one on the history of political philosophy from Plato through Mao. I had no particular devotion to Mao; he just happened to be the last major figure to come along in the 2,000 plus years of political thought I was exploring. The dean of my faculty possessed a copy of my syllabus and had posed no objection. Even more to the point, my class had only just finished studying Nicolo Machiavelli—the famous Italian Renaissance thinker whose amoral political counsel my students considered particularly helpful in understanding how their own authoritarian government worked.

We were now considering Thomas Hobbes, a seventeenth century British philosopher whose famous work, *Leviathan*, justified a powerful state. The students wouldn't even get to the twentieth century and Mao for several weeks. I had recently delivered two of Mao's short essays to the university printer, asking that they be mimeographed within a month so I could then distribute them to my students. "Just check back with the printer," I pleaded with my listeners. My rationalist defense, however, evoked only a few sighs of resignation.

I don't remember how I got back to our faculty garden apartment three miles across town. All I can recall were the worrisome questions coursing through my brain: "How can I tell Nancy that we have to pick up and leave our home for the last fifteen months immediately?" . . . "Will she be angry and ask a lot of questions I can't answer?" . . . "How will she react to the threat of my arrest now hanging over our family?"

A feeling of guilt began to weigh me down. I was the supposedly knowledgeable twenty-eight-year-old "Africanist" who had persuaded my twenty-two-year-old wife to leave her known world of New York City, including her close family, to spend two academic years in the most battle-scarred city in Sub-Saharan Africa.

The terrible civil war that had killed tens of thousands of people, including many in and around the rebel capital of Kisangani, had largely ended only four years earlier. The very building I taught in was pockmarked with bullet holes. It was popularly called the "Six Codo" (6th Commando), after the White mercenary-led army unit that had mutinied and seized Kisangani three years earlier. Now we were being forced out of our home and God knew what "justice" might await us in the capital, Kinshasa. Would I be arrested and jailed like the seven alleged student "ringleaders" or the American professor who had tried to take pictures of the apologizing students? Would we be summarily deported?

I raced up the stairs to our second floor flat overlooking a stately palm forest. Rushing through the living and dining rooms, past the kitchen entrance where our cook Michel was cleaning up, I found Nancy taking a bath. Breathing rapidly, sweat dripping from my forehead, I knocked and pushed open the bathroom door. Nancy was sitting peacefully in the tub. For a few seconds all I could do was lean against the bathroom door and gaze at her. Nancy raised her eyes nonchalantly. Straightening myself and preparing to speak, I felt my lips curl into the awkward smile I sometimes form when I'm uncomfortable.

"I don't want you to be upset," I began slowly, "but something happened at the meeting this morning that affects us." Nancy rose slowly and began drying herself as if I weren't there. Her beautiful sky-blue eyes had not yet fully opened. She was still inhabiting the dreamy world of The Bath. With a rising urgency in my voice, I began to recount the ministers' decisions. Nancy stood quietly, holding tightly the towel she had wrapped around herself. When I had finished, she asked, innocently, "Why, what have we done?" I put my arm around her. "It's not you, it's me," I said. "I was seen talking to the students. They think I'm involved in the boycott."

Pulling away, I tried to reassure Nancy by drawing upon my endless well of rationalist optimism: "I'm sure the university sold the ministers a bill of goods," I observed. "Before we leave, I'll send telegrams to the American Embassy in Kinshasa and Alfred Cahen (a top official in the Belgian Embassy who'd come to lunch at our house). Everything will be OK." This was actually what I half-believed.

The regular Air Congo flight from Kisangani to the Congolese capital was scheduled to leave at 4:30 p.m. We had to tell Daniel about our departure calmly enough to not frighten him. Nancy called me into his bedroom where he was playing with Michel's wife, Marie, who took care of him in the mornings. We told him we were going for a trip in an airplane. We were leaving Kisangani, after saying goodbye to everyone, and would see grandma and grandpa in the United States very soon. Daniel's eyes grew wide. He turned our words into questions, forcing us to repeat them so he could take it all in.

We tried to explain the situation to Marie—an attractive young woman with hair rolled up in several tight sticks in the Congolese style—but she understood little of our French. That was the lingua franca of the well-educated. She grasped enough though to walk quickly into the kitchen and get Michel. As we talked to him, the lines on his intelligent face seemed to deepen and his eyes glanced back and forth between Nancy and me. As Nancy later wrote in her journal, "The careful mask of the agreeable servant fell." Michel Okenge had so much to lose. He was about my age. The fifteen months he'd spent with us had been his first steady job after years of deprivation. During the 1964 rebellions and subsequent repression by White mercenaries and government troops, he had fled into the forest, nearly starving to death. Although he could now afford to eat regularly, he told us he took but one meal a day, "just in case" events turned on him again.

Seeing the anxiety on his grown-up companion's face, Daniel walked over and leaned his small body on his leg. Michel lifted him up into his arms. Pulling himself together, he spoke gently to Daniel in the Swahili he had patiently taught him over the months.

We wanted to say something to relieve Michel's fear, but quickly realized how helpless we were. Kisangani, the third largest city in the Congo, was teeming with unemployment and poverty. Beggars, often severely deformed, greeted you as you entered shops. Walking down the road, passing children might sing you a refrain from a popular song: "*Mundele, donnez-moi la caisse*"—literally, "European, give me your cash box"—as they extended their hands for money.

Nancy told Michel to keep the bicycle they had shared and take all our food home. Later, when we packed, we gave Michel and Marie anything they could use and all the cash we could spare. Our friends Alistair and Mary promised to try to find Michel another job at the university.

Alistair offered to drive Nancy to the *Lycée* Virgo Immaculata, the girls' Catholic high school run by Franciscan missionary nuns where she had taught English for a year. On the way, Nancy's characteristically gentle public presentation evaporated. As she wrote in her journal several years later:

I felt my anxiety swell until, like a river, it threatened to overflow and drown everyone near it. In a surge of rage, I bitterly attacked everyone and everything that I thought might be to blame for our predicament. "What could you expect in a country where even the postal clerks were corrupt? There is no free speech here. In the President's so-called free election last year everyone was forced to vote and given only one choice. People are still executed in public hangings, for God's sake, and the whole city is forced from their homes to watch. And what about us? We get good salaries and "houseboys," we're treated like millionaires, while my students still live in huts without electricity and water. They do their work by kerosene lamps or fires, but what support do they get? Even the university's students have to scramble for books, and they just had their food ration cut again. We're their only hope to escape poverty." The more I shouted, the more I could contain my fear, as though anger were turning my anxiety into strength.

Alistair, a man of saintly patience, was shaken by Nancy's outburst. Arriving at the mission, tears streaming down her cheeks, Nancy passed her books and papers to the Mother Superior. Worried that her senior students would lose ground in preparing for the state examinations, which would go far toward determining their futures, she suggested a recently arrived young American woman as her possible replacement. Taking Nancy's hand, the head of the female religious community assured her, in a choked voice, "I will pray for you."

As we hurriedly packed, there was a tentative knock at the front door. It was one of my Congolese faculty colleagues, come to say farewell. We spoke about our fears for the arrested students. One by one, several other American, African, and European friends ventured to our apartment. They told us that many others wanted to come but were afraid they were being watched by security police. Quietly, they shook our hands, murmured a few words of encouragement, and departed.

Finally, Nancy's senior English class arrived, led by the school's principal, Sister Francine. They had walked the few miles from the school that Nancy had traversed daily on her bike. The girls were dressed in their blue and white uniforms and barefoot. Sister Francine wore her long black habit. Nancy's students could not let her leave without personally saying farewell.

Leaving most of our possessions behind for later shipping, we hurried to the airport only to learn that the Air Congo flight to Kinshasa had been canceled. Overwhelmed by the speed of the government's crackdown, we had forgotten about its customary inefficiency. Marooned at the airport, we were rescued by a warm, young American couple, U.S. Information Agency officer Bob Palmeri and his wife Fran.

Earlier that day, I'd gotten a message to Bob, the only representative of the U.S. government on the scene, asking him to alert the embassy in Kinshasa and our Belgian friend Cahen of our impending arrival. I requested that we be met at the airport "because of possible arrest situation." Although we knew Bob and Fran only slightly, they had shown up for our departure and offered to put us up for the night in their luxurious, air-conditioned apartment in Kisangani's tallest building—the twelve-story "Immoquateur." After fifteen months on the equator without even a fan, it was quite a treat. They moved into the vacationing U.S. consul's flat.

The next afternoon we met Alistair and Mary for lunch at the Olympia Greek restaurant. It happened to be Nancy's twenty-fourth birthday. Returning to the airport, we awaited our departure on a bench. Michel arrived with his hand enveloped by the biggest bandage I had ever seen. I had two thoughts: "Oh my gosh, what happened to him?" and "This is just part of all this wackiness!" While assuring us he'd be

```
94cabpbl kgn
386 amem kin
94cabpbl kgn


kisangani, le 27 mars 1971.-


ambassade americain telex 386 kinshasa.-


immediate 139 from kisangani 26
march twenty seven
university professor stephen weissman, american citizen,
being expelled from kisangani by order of vice minister of
interior presently here investigating university situation.
arriving kinshasa today on qo405 at 1930 with wife and small
child. he has been ordered to report to ministry of interior.
request that he be met because of possible arrest situation.-

   palmeri ++

termine avez vous bien recu??

 ok well received this aneb kin 386

386 amem kinv



tace  taxe 4 mnts+
```

Cable sent at author's request from U.S. Consulate, Kisangani, to American Embassy, Kinshasa, re: author's expulsion from University.

fine, Michel recounted how a pig at the market had bitten him. Several of my students, who lived at the main university dormitory across from the airport, took the chance of stopping by to express their sympathy.

At one point, Vice-Rector A appeared, not as I first guessed to regretfully see us off, but to meet someone else. As he moved by the waiting passengers, he paused to shake hands with those he knew. I braced myself to accept his greeting. I thought, "Look, he was undoubtedly part of the group that has done this to us, but I can't hold him mainly responsible because he has always seemed so ineffectual." He arrived first in front of

Nancy. *"Bonjour, Madame,"* he said, smilingly, extending his hand. Nancy simply stared at him. He left his hand out for an uncomfortable number of seconds before giving up and presenting it to me: *"Bonjour, Monsieur."* He smiled again, as if I were the kind of man who would undermine his wife just to please him. I turned away.

Nancy's cold-shouldering of the vice-rector surprised me. The face she showed in public settings was invariably one of politeness and warmth. Her unexpected reaction revealed not only her simmering anger, but also her authenticity and clarity of judgment.

When we landed in Kinshasa, there were thankfully no Congolese police on hand to greet us. Nor, however, were there any American or Belgian diplomats to protect and counsel us. (Later, I learned that Cahen had showed up, but we had missed him because our plane arrived very early and we weren't keeping track of the time.) Somewhat dejectedly, we boarded a taxi to the Mennonite-run guesthouse where we had stayed upon our arrival in the Congo. With its quiet, somewhat dark rooms and silent meals, it provided us with a refuge that felt both ethereally calm and worryingly transient.

Why was this happening to us? I wondered. Was the president's intelligence agency so paranoid that a few pages of Mao's writings for a political science course and being seen talking to a couple of striking students I encountered on campus were perceived as subversion? Or was I mostly a convenient scapegoat for a group of fearful university bureaucrats trying to cover their asses before an authoritarian regime that had grown anxious about continuing student unrest at the university? Had I carelessly helped undermine us by my earlier expressions of sympathy for a militant Congolese student, faculty, and staff movement for more Black power over the university? And why hadn't the American Embassy responded to my concern that I might be arrested upon landing in the capital?

As the days and years went by, I would find myself pondering a more profound and troubling issue. Having parachuted into a rather murky and suddenly racially fraught environment, had I overindulged my American, 1960s-era values and sympathies? Had I failed to adequately gauge the potential consequences of taking certain risks in a foreign country that, notwithstanding my extensive academic research, I only thought I understood? Had I carelessly placed my family in jeopardy?

~~~

CHAPTER 2

CHILDREN OF THE 1960S
VENTURE INTO AFRICA

~~~

To *begin to understand* what was happening to us, it is helpful to know some things about my personal background, the history of post-independence Congo, and our experience of Kisangani—the most fascinating place I have ever lived.

Two days before the end of the 1960s, after flying for three hours in a small propeller plane over an endless green forest, we landed in Kisangani. Our decision to live and work there for two years was mainly the product of a researcher's curiosity about his subject.

I had begun working on my dissertation in 1966. My interest in the Congo had been nourished by the era's broader questioning of America's racial and foreign policies. What were the deeper reasons, I had wondered, behind the United States's ongoing plunge into the war in distant South Vietnam, including its carpet bombing of Asian civilians commonly derided as "gooks"? To gain more perspective, I had decided to study America's simultaneous political and military intervention on a different, racially distinct, continent, Africa. I hoped that my analysis of the Congo case would provide useful insights into the roots and consequences of American diplomacy.

The Democratic Republic of the Congo is the largest country in Sub-Saharan Africa and one of the richest in natural resources. It's where the U.S. acquired the uranium for its first atomic bombs (it was then called the Belgium Congo) and where various minerals in Americans' cell phones and electric cars come from today. It had been a major focus of Cold War conflict, though one that had drawn little public attention. Indeed, G. Mennen Williams, the former assistant secretary of state for Africa during the John F. Kennedy administration, later told me that when he took office in 1961, "There was talk of sending troops. . . . The Congo was bigger than Vietnam."[1] In studying this case, I was betting that the recent ebbing of the Congo crisis, together with the fact that it had not attracted much public controversy, would encourage the American officials I hoped to interview to be relatively candid.

Nancy and I had met in September 1965 while volunteering in liberal Democratic Congressman William F. Ryan's campaign for mayor of New York. She was from Brooklyn and performed folk songs at campaign rallies. She opened for the legendary Pete Seeger the evening we first noticed each other. I was from Queens and spouted off about Ryan's virtues on sound trucks. I got to accompany such luminaries as actress Rita Moreno and civil rights leader James Farmer. Nancy and I fell in love and were married in March 1967.

At that time, I was an instructor in American government on the Bronx campus of Jesuit-run Fordham University while working on my thesis. These were turbulent times at American universities.

By the end of 1968, I had become one of the leaders of two overlapping student-faculty movements at Fordham. The first focused on three issues: ending the Jesuit order's (but not lay Catholics') control of the university's Board of Trustees in order to obtain New York State financial aid, broadening student and faculty representation in educational decisions, and ending racism by raising Black and Puerto Rican student admissions to 20 percent (only 1 percent of the students were African Americans) and instituting a Black Studies program. The second movement sought to abolish the campus Reserve Officers Training Program (ROTC). Many ROTC courses smacked of political indoctrination into militant Cold War foreign policy rather than free, academic inquiry. More compellingly, the training program was a direct university contribution to what we believed to be an unjust war in Vietnam. Our movements employed a variety of protest techniques including petitions, public demonstrations, teach-ins, sit-ins, and sleep-ins in university buildings.

My political persona at Fordham was hardly that of the stereotypical "1960s radical." I did not belong to any political organization. While expressing my views forthrightly, I favored reasoned, patient argument. For example, I wrote a series of articles for the student newspaper criticizing the academic quality of ROTC course materials. Moreover, I supported the formation of broad coalitions to achieve practical objectives. Thus, I worked hard to reconcile the positions of members of the leftist Students for a Democratic Society, pro-Eugene McCarthy and Robert Kennedy Democratic Party liberals, libertarians, and independents). I was also determined to maintain relations with those with whom we disagreed.

21

Although our groups directly confronted the university administration, Fordham's top leaders had a sense of the times. They gave the appearance of listening seriously to us and avoiding unnecessary overreactions to our passionate actions. My most difficult moment came in the spring of 1969 when over 100 of us occupied the president's outer office in an anti-ROTC protest. The demonstration was arguably non-disruptive since the secretaries in the area continued to do their work. After twenty-four hours, however, the university obtained a temporary court injunction against the demonstrators, forcing us out. The target of the injunction, which I received under our Bronx apartment door, was "Steve Weissman et al." As I emerged from the building and made my way to my office, I bumped into Father James Finlay, my rather liberal department chairman who later became Fordham's president. He thanked me for discouraging my co-demonstrators from rifling through the administration's file cabinets. (Evidently the administration had a spy in our ranks!) Fordham could have readily gotten rid of me then as my teaching contract was concluding. Instead, it gave me a new, two-year appointment as an assistant professor. Subsequently, it granted me leaves of absence to teach in the Congo.

Contemplating our forthcoming trip, I breathed a sigh of relief. Nationally, the student movement was becoming more frustrated and militant under President Richard Nixon's unresponsive administration. If I stayed at Fordham, our groups, it seemed to me, would come under pressure to undertake ever riskier, more obstructive actions that were unlikely to accomplish much. In fact, that was exactly what happened. In November 1969, students seized the administration building to protest ROTC; twenty-one were arrested and charged with criminal trespass. Most accepted a deal that included a period of court supervision, but five chose to stand trial, were convicted, and received suspended sentences. Avoiding such risky choices, I was now headed for the Protestant-sponsored ULC as a "Government Technical Assistant" paid by the Ministry of Education, intending only to teach and learn.

I was fully informed about the country's authoritarian political system. Indeed, I had spent four years studying how my government, guided by a misplaced anti-communism stance, had helped establish that system from 1960 through 1964.[2] My thesis, later revised and published by Cornell University Press, contained the first scholarly account of the role of the U.S. Central Intelligence Agency (CIA) in the overthrow of Patrice Lumumba, the Congo's first democratically elected prime minister. It traced the consolidation of power by the U.S.-promoted "Binza Group," of which Colonel Joseph Mobutu was the most important figure. And it portrayed the Congo government's bloody repression of subsequent Lumumbist rebellions with decisive assistance from the CIA and Belgium.

By mid-summer of 1960, U.S. President Dwight Eisenhower and his top advisors had become convinced that Lumumba, who was maneuvering to recover the Congo's richest province, which had seceded with Belgian assistance, was "serving Soviet purposes." They saw the relatively inexperienced, mercurial young leader as being egged on by "anti-Western" and "Communist" advisors to replace a United Nations Peacekeeping force that refused to subdue Katanga with Soviet Bloc military assistance. They decided that the U.S. should "get rid of" Lumumba lest the Congo turn Communist. Scholars and declassified Soviet Bloc archives have shown, however, that these fears were highly exaggerated.

While exploring various assassination schemes, the U.S. joined Belgium in sponsoring and guiding political opposition to Lumumba. Within weeks, CIA station chief Larry Devlin— as he later testified to a Senate investigating committee—had "arranged and supported, and indeed managed" a military coup by the twenty-nine-year-old Sergeant-Major turned Colonel, Mobutu. The latter had previously been a journalist and close aide to Lumumba. Although Mobutu was reliably anti-Soviet, Devlin often found him difficult to manage and subject to periods of depression.

To support Mobutu and his close allies—known as the Binza Group after the Leopoldville suburb where most of them lived—the CIA secretly spent over $90 to $150 million in current dollars from 1960 through 1968. Those figures do not count the substantial aircraft, weapons, transportation, and maintenance services transferred to the covert operations by the Defense Department.

During most of this period, the CIA had a hand in every major political turning point, most notably in the assassination of Lumumba in January 1961. As the threat of an army mutiny to restore the imprisoned prime minister grew, Mobutu and others on the CIA payroll decided to transfer him to secessionist leaders who had vowed to kill him. Devlin, who had previously, at the request of his superiors, explored nine different ways of assassinating Lumumba, was informed of the plan in advance and raised no objection. Not only that. He withheld his knowledge of the plan from Washington for three days until Lumumba had been shipped to Katanga, where he was promptly murdered.

In 1964, the U.S. stepped in strongly, as Lumumbist rebels, with modest Chinese advisory and financial assistance, challenged the failing civilian government. The CIA fielded an "instant Air Force" of planes, pilots, and maintenance facilities and personnel that enabled Mobutu's troops, led by hundreds of brutal White mercenaries, to subdue and terrorize rebel-held areas. It has been estimated that tens of thousands of Congolese perished during the rebellions, mainly rebels and civilians indiscriminately slaughtered by the government's forces.

In 1965, Mobutu dispensed with his principal civilian collaborators, grabbing sole power as president. This second coup was facilitated by a wink and a nod from Devlin.

By the time I arrived in December 1969, the rebellions had been defeated. Prices for Congo's minerals had been rising for three straight years and the government had carried out a successful currency reform. Mobutu had succeeded in coopting several potential opponents into his regime, ranging from former Binza Group colleagues to leftist student leaders. With peace restored, it appeared to many observers that the president's rule was broadly accepted, even popular in some places. At the same time, there was no doubt that this was an authoritarian regime that had dissolved parliament and dealt ruthlessly with real and suspected opponents.

I also knew that Mobutu's army had killed between 40 and 100 Lovanium University students in Kinshasa in June 1969. They had attempted to march through the city to back demands to improve their conditions of study after the government broke its earlier promise to give them an independent voice in their education. However, to my mind, the capital was 1,800 miles from Kisangani, and I had no intention of getting involved in any challenge to the government.

It was Wilbert LeMelle Sr, head of the Ford Foundation's Africa Program, who originally put me in touch with the ULC, which had been established in 1963 but had functioned uninterrupted by violence for only one year. I had met Wilbert through his twin brother, Tilden, a political science colleague at Fordham who was a pioneering analyst of the domestic and international Black Power movements.

I had mentioned to Tilden my interest in teaching in the Congo. As it happened, Wilbert had recently met with one of the American missionaries who led the university's administration. The LeMelles said they knew of no major issue of academic freedom at ULC. Their view seemed further confirmed when I got to the university and met Tom Turner, a graduate student from the University of Wisconsin. His appointment had been facilitated by Professor M. Crawford Young, the "dean" of U.S. scholars of Congo politics.

I was excited by the prospect of living in the former Stanleyville. Beyond its exotic location and storied colonial past, the city had been Lumumba's political base and the capital of the populist 1964 Eastern Rebellion. However, Nancy looked at the prospect of leaving her family and friends for a mysterious city in the heart of the African continent with some trepidation. Still, after graduating from college and spending most of the next two years at home caring for baby Daniel and supporting my exploits, she admitted she was getting bored. She had not yet decided among various potential careers, including singing, social work, and teaching. I assured her that, based on my conversations with scholars who had taught in Africa, we would likely have a wonderful, eye-opening experience and she was certain to find useful work. And we would have more time to spend together as a family.

Our journey was delayed for three nerve-wracking months due to a financial dispute between Belgian and Congolese airlines. At last, we received our tickets from New York to Brussels via Sabena and onward to Kinshasa via Air Congo. The latter flight stopped in Rome, where a large number of Italians and Congolese joined us. With French, Italian, and African languages streaming from all quarters, and numerous babies on hand, we had a comforting feeling of international community.

During the trip, we looked down upon the lovely, forbidding Sahara Desert for what seemed like hours. Finally, under a bright afternoon sun, we descended over the greenest forest I had ever seen, passed quickly over the mud-brown Congo River, and landed in Kinshasa. It was Christmas Eve.

A university driver took us to the *Union Mission Hospitalière,* a guest house run by the American Mennonite Central Committee. Most of the residents were serious young people who traveled to rural areas to establish schools and teach. Although we were scheduled to fly to Kisangani the following day, Daniel came down with the flu, his temperature soaring to 105 degrees. Fortunately, an American doctor from the same clinic that President Mobutu used came to our cabin and prescribed an antibiotic. Nancy also became ill. While our family recovered, we acclimated to the unfamiliar Mennonite custom of silence during meals.

After five days, we flew to Kisangani. Upon arriving "with all the grace that a crying child, six overflowing overnight bags and a guitar allowed," as Nancy later wrote, we were briefly greeted by top university officials. We quickly understood that they were really at the airport to receive the visiting minister of education. Dropped off at a university guest house, we were invited to lunch and dinner by the head of the university's health service, a pleasant American missionary doctor. Relaxing with the Olson family in their comfortable home gave us the strange feeling that we had suddenly left Africa and been transported back to a small American city in Minnesota. For supper, there was macaroni and cheese, passed around on Melmac plates. The living room had a window air conditioner and a Christmas tree with imitation snow. After dinner, Dr. Olson sat back, turned on the radio and we all listened to the Voice of America.

Our first year in Kisangani seemed to validate my optimism. While we were uncomfortable with certain aspects of our life there, we were mainly enthralled. It felt like we were truly *in* Africa. There were, according to official statistics, more than 200,000 people in the city, comprising fewer than 600 Europeans (including Americans), a fifth of whom were associated with the university. There were also 300 non-Congolese Africans and a number of Asians, mostly Pakistanis.

The town's center was lovely. The main roads were lined with rows of tall, perfectly spaced palm trees. There were several striking squares. One was especially pretty with its short, head-high palms laid out in triangular formations and framed by majestic shaded walks. A discordant sign indicated that soldiers had been "savagely murdered" there during the 1964 rebellion. It was the site of the former Lumumba monument where enemies of the rebellion were publicly executed.

Every time I mounted the steps of the rich yellow post office with its deep blue columns—and that was often since Kisangani had no mailboxes—I felt uplifted. Private homes, former Belgian colonial villas now occupied by the town's Congolese and foreign elite and some squatters, were painted in multi-hued tropical colors and enveloped by attractive gardens. There were almost no tall buildings to distract you from the way the sun, more brilliant than I'd ever seen it, animated the lush vegetation. Everywhere there were fresh smells (including that of sweat generated by the ever-present humidity). Walking through the big open-air central market, you could bargain with women traders for say, live chickens and the sweetest pineapples, or snack on *makate*—orange-brown balls of fried dough—or freshly made peanut butter wrapped in a bright green leaf. You could also wander among streets with dozens of largely Greek and Pakistani-owned shops selling imported goods, vegetables, bread, pastries, and meats, not to mention the services of carpenters, tailors, and barbers. I was often reminded of the towns in old "Western" movies with their sun-bleached, sandy streets, small stores, and vagabond chickens. Some of the shops had bullet holes from past violence and a number had been burnt out.

Flowing past the Western edge of the main city was the great, mud-tinted Congo River. You could take a *pirogue* (a sturdy canoe made from a tree trunk) across to the left bank, picnic with friends, as we did once with a Congolese agricultural engineer and his Belgian wife, and lazily watch the Wagenia fishermen, who built complex structures of long wooden sticks over the rapids to support their nets, performing delicate maneuvers atop the swirling waters.

Our home was a charming faculty and higher administrator-occupied apartment complex located up an unpaved road about a mile from downtown. There were nine three-story buildings, spread out in a well-spaced circle with plenty of green grass in the middle. Each *Bloc Universitaire* contained six comfortable, simply furnished one- and two-bedroom apartments for individuals and small families. (A minority of faculty and top administrators, most with larger families, inhabited private villas across town near the university). A few pillars still bore the scrawls of the White mercenaries who had mutinied in 1966 and 1967.

From our large second floor windows and terrace we looked out on tall palm trees. They swayed like dancers in the sudden winds that preceded the occasional, brief thunderstorm. Sometimes after the rain stopped, thousands of flying insects would attempt to squeeze through our windows, and we would wear out our fly swatter. One species of flying ant calmly walked out of their shells after we bashed them. At night we saw lights from downtown and listened to the friendly chatter of birds and crickets and the distant beating of village drums.

After Michel made lunch, the main meal of the day, Nancy and I would retire to our bedroom, make love and nap, escaping the midday heat and humidity. Daniel took a siesta too. Wakened by cooling breezes, we would venture out for a late afternoon family stroll. On some afternoons, I would hoist Daniel up on my shoulders and walk the three miles to the university to pick up our mail. We usually rode home in the

Our home in the Blocs Universitaires *with Daniel in the foreground.*

university's Volkswagen Kombi microbus which shuttled to and from the *Blocs*. Some evenings, Nancy and I would walk down the dark, peaceful unpaved road to the city center, the moon obscured by the whispering palms on either side of us. We sorrowfully relinquished this pleasure when enough people had warned us it was unsafe, though we never actually heard about any violent incident.

Our small, mainly expatriate enclave exuded a pleasing communal atmosphere. We were American, Dutch, Congolese (the three largest components of the teaching and administrative staff), French, Belgian, Spanish, West African, British, Swiss, Indian, South Vietnamese, and more. With no television, poor radio reception, a lone telephone in the *Blocs* for emergencies, only a handful of nearby restaurants, and few cultural events, we invited each other over for dinner. When you felt like chatting with someone, you simply showed up at their door and they would invariably invite you in for a cold Primus or Stanor beer and fresh peanuts.

We did discover one enormously attractive destination: the Olympia Hotel and Restaurant, owned by a Greek Cypriot and his British wife. Besides delicious Greek food, it offered a magical outdoor space where you could eat, drink, and dance to Congolese and international music played by "Garcia's Rock n' Band." Framed by palm trees and illuminated by colored fluorescent lights, the "garden" seated hundreds of customers beside a circular dance floor. In her University of Manchester doctoral thesis on "Relations between Europeans and Zairians in the city of Kisangani," my colleague, social anthropologist Ruth Kornfield-Gilman, described the interesting cultural/racial dynamic that played out nightly:

This was a popular drinking place for both Zairians and Europeans, but they used it differently. In the early hours of the evening, the clientele was predominately European, and the music played by the orchestra was Greek or Belgian and there was little dancing. At ten o'clock, the orchestra began playing Afro-American and Zairian dance music, the garden began to fill up with Zairians and the Europeans began to leave. By midnight there would be a large number of Zairians drinking and dancing and only a few remaining Europeans.[3]

I remember Pierre Kazadi, one of our Congolese acquaintances who was a musicologist, introducing Nancy to the Congolese version of the rumba, with its subtle and precise swaying of the hips. Our expeditions to the Olympia increased our appreciation of Congolese music, ever present on the radio and popular throughout Africa. Marrying South American rhythms to African ones, it built upon traditional African instruments and was constantly innovating. A highlight of our stay in Kisangani was the Olympia appearance of the famous singer Tabu Ley Rochereau and his band, including their dancing "Rochelettes," reminiscent of the young women who performed with Ray Charles and James Brown.

From time to time, we would be stirred by an unexpected public event. One afternoon, strolling through the city center, we heard the sound of drums and came upon a large group of people outside a villa observing a man with a white-painted face dancing in a circle. He was bare-chested, adorned with an elaborate white necklace, and wore a traditional men's long white skirt. Perhaps his most striking feature was a large headdress packed with feathers. A man who was leading him in the dance explained to us that he had lost his memory and the purpose of the rite was to restore it.

Another time, the world-famous anthropologist Colin Turnbull visited the university on his way to study Pygmies in Northeastern Congo. Unhappily, his timing was such that he was requisitioned by the provincial governor to attend a public hanging of two robbers. From the hill adjoining our home, I could see the outline of the event—but fortunately not the details.

In advance of the 1970 elections, in which he was the only presidential candidate, Mobutu paid a visit to Kisangani. The city center benefited from an impromptu paint job. The president held a public campaign meeting, which I attended. Speaking Lingala, which I did not understand, he seemed to be energetic and in good humor. I was surprised that the crowd, hoisting their umbrellas against the brutal afternoon sun, offered no discernible reactions to his words.

Within weeks of our arrival, Nancy had joined a chorale in our *Blocs Universitaires*, was playing her guitar with a Spanish composer and a Congolese musician, and was participating in a modern dance class led by a fellow American married to my Guinean dean. Nancy was also a big hit at a university talent show in our second year, singing in French and English. I was moved when the largely non-English-speaking Congolese audience began to sing along with her during the African American spiritual "Wade in the Water."

With a nearby sandbox, volleyball court, ample grass, and the opportunity to swap toys from various countries, Daniel frolicked with about five times more playmates in the *Blocs* than he had in New York City. They were mainly Congolese, Scottish, West African, Belgian, French, American, and Dutch. While we taught him English, he picked up large swatches of Swahili, Lingala, and French from the other kids and their Congolese nannies. Within a few months he had become our sometime Swahili interpreter with the many locals who did not speak French.

In addition to Alistair and Mary, we were particularly friendly with Mado, a beautiful and vivacious Parisian, formerly a French teacher. Nancy and Mado exchanged English and French lessons. Mado's adorable children, Sara and Yacub, were Daniel's favorite playmates. Mado's husband Moussa, a tall, smiling Malian professor, once barbecued a sheep outside for our community during the Muslim festival of the Eid. Moussa kindly offered me the delicacy of the animal's testicles, which I squeamishly declined. When I finally decided, at the ripe age of twenty-nine, to learn to ride a bicycle, Mado came out to watch me practice on the dirt road that wound around the *Bloc* and cheered me on.

However, while pregnant with her third child, Mado discovered that Moussa had been unfaithful. After throwing him out of their apartment, she took her revenge by getting him fired from our moralistic Protestant university, thereby eliminating her main source of income. Shortly afterward, a Congolese law professor and I spent a couple of hours talking her out of committing suicide. With her frantic monologue straining my adequate but not quite fluent French, I was grateful for Monsieur Mbila's presence. What if I had been alone with her, missed some crucial point, and she had carried out her passionate threat? After Mado gave birth in Paris (due to inadequate medical facilities expatriates generally had their children abroad), she returned to Kisangani. Since she and her children were no longer eligible for faculty housing, she moved into the city center. After we left Kisangani, we heard she had gone to Kinshasa and secured a secretarial position in a Western embassy.

We encountered one other case of domestic discord veering toward self-destruction. A Congolese neighbor, an administrator, separated from his wife because he did not believe the child she was bearing was his. According to his ethnic tradition, a man had to have sexual relations with a woman several times within a short period of time to impregnate her. Since he did not want a third child, he had limited intercourse with his wife to once a month. When she nonetheless became pregnant, he accused her of having slept with another man while he was away on a business trip. She insisted upon her fidelity. Their families did not quarrel with his view of pregnancy but argued that he was at fault for leaving such a pretty young woman alone and should take her back. Instead, he left his wife with her family in Kinshasa and took their children with him to Kisangani. All she could do was wait, hoping that her husband would take her back.

Like other professors, we hired a "cook." Michel was a thin, good-looking man with a small mustache. Not only did he prepare most of our meals, he also shopped, cleaned, washed, and ironed. (You couldn't hang clothes outside to dry lest they attract worms that would savage your skin.) Relatively well educated—he had nearly finished high school—Michel was thoughtful and had a good sense of humor. To us, he was much more than a "boy," the humiliating but still widely used colonial term for men who did domestic work. Michel was our main window onto local Congolese society, from which we were quite isolated. In the end, he would be the Congolese with whom we felt closest.

Grateful to be working after years of privation, Michel was happy to answer all our questions. From him that we learned that Congolese had to pay bribes to get their prescriptions filled at clinics and that, before the single-candidate presidential "election," the Swahili language radio station warned, "No one knows what is going to happen to those who vote 'Red' instead of (the preferred) 'Green'." Nancy heard the same message delivered at an official pre-election meeting she attended. Other Congolese informed us that Green ballots were often unavailable at the polls.

Michel also showed Nancy the scar on the back of his neck where his mother had inserted burnt herbs to protect him from demons.

Most mornings he brought us delicious papayas he picked on his way to work. And he introduced us to delectable Congolese dishes like manioc leaves in palm oil. Michel had a particular affection for Daniel, teaching him Swahili and pulling him along on his Italian-made tricycle as he biked down the hill to shop at the grand African market.

After several months, we observed that Michel's relationship with Marie was deteriorating. Every couple of weeks they would come in, obviously miserable with each other. He had taken a second wife, which was not uncommon, and claimed that she was jealous. We wondered whether Marie's failure to conceive a child had played a role. Sometimes Marie had a black eye or swollen mouth. Michel claimed that she insulted him in front of friends and even tried to poison him. We couldn't learn Marie's side of the story because she spoke mainly Swahili. After a while, we told them that they needed to avoid any suggestion of marital tension in front of Daniel, or we'd be compelled to let them go. They observed a cease-fire.

Notwithstanding the fascinating environment, we were always uneasy living as members of an elite in an overwhelmingly poor, beaten down city. The beggars we encountered almost every day were particularly sad. Many had missing, deformed, or atrophied limbs from war and disease. Almost 85 percent of the Congolese lived, as they had in colonial times, in six outlying "communes" where no Whites dwelled and few worked.

A couple of times we took the long walk across the Tshopo River Bridge to the neighborhood where Michel and Marie lived. We visited the home they shared with three others: a one room house with no mattresses, electricity, or running water and an outdoor "kitchen." There we came face to face with the poverty that was all around us. What a depressing contrast with the lavish outdoor dinner that Provincial Governor Edouard Bulundwe had recently thrown for the university faculty, with mosquitoes landing in our champagne glasses.

Despite our discomfort, Nancy and I felt that, through our jobs, we were helping hundreds of young people, and perhaps eventually the society itself, to move forward.

I particularly enjoyed teaching my large introductory political science course. Initially, I focused on helping students comprehend the post-independence developments that they had personally lived through. In accordance with advice I had received from my colleagues and the administration, I discussed

*Daniel and his caregiver, Marie, pausing to rest at a bar in
Tshopo Commune, Kisangani. (Nancy and I were with them.)
The pourer is wearing the shirt of the Popular Revolutionary
Movement (MRP) the only legal political party.*

the ins and outs of recent Congo politics factually without
saying anything negative about Mobutu or his regime. While
I did not ignore the U.S. role, I consciously played it down.

Sometimes my students' responses were both surprising and
instructive. Once, I related how rural rebels with bows and
arrows had been accompanied by traditional "healers" who
promised that, if certain taboos were observed, the bullets of

White mercenaries and Congolese troops would turn to water. When that did not happen, the rebels were overwhelmed by forces brandishing modern weapons. But one of my students raised his hand and said he had personally observed bullets turning into water. No one in the class evinced any reaction to his comment. I could not—and therefore did not—dispute my student's strongly held perception.

I was proud of having divided one of my classes into six research groups, meeting weekly with each of them. I showed the students how to develop and administer questionnaires that were based partly on their intimate knowledge of Congolese society. How else would I have known, for example, that an important indicator of higher social class in the Congo was possession of a tin roof? With permissions I obtained from the provincial government, the students conducted interviews surveying the educational and professional background of provincial officials, the class status and household budgets of average families, and the professional aspirations and political ideologies of their colleagues. The students manifested considerable initiative and flexibility, artfully navigating problems that rarely came up in American research, such as their respondents' requests for beers in exchange for answers.

My heart went out to these men and few women, many in their mid-twenties with spouses and children, whose attentiveness and capacities were not very different from those I had taught at Fordham—a reasonably selective university that attracted many of the best graduates of New York's Catholic high schools. Some, though, were clearly distracted by their material privations: small scholarships, poor housing, skimpy food. Withal, I was struck by how grateful the students were for their educational opportunity. In the absence of books, many would stand on line outside the puny school library, waiting to read chapters from French language books I had purchased from Europe. Mercifully, they were patient and helpful as my spoken French improved. Although I had minored in French literature in college, I initially possessed limited experience in conversation.

At the same time, I felt strangely cut off from them. Like the other professors, I lacked an office to meet with students. The university had no student union or common restaurant where we might get together informally. On our spread-out campus, students usually had to run for a bus to their next class or to their distant residence, so there was little time to linger for a chat. Moreover, they generally lived about four miles from the *Blocs* and lacked transportation.

Since I had come to the Congo for purely educational reasons, I never discussed contemporary politics with my students. On one occasion though, I got a hint of the latent dissatisfaction and the nationalist militancy to come.

On the ninth anniversary of Lumumba's assassination, the student branch of the government-mandated single political party, the Popular Revolutionary Movement or MPR, held a public meditation for the fallen leader. Despite his role in Lumumba's overthrow and murder, Mobutu had declared Lumumba a "national hero" as he sought to assume his nationalist mantle.

Of course, I decided to attend. At first, it seemed that the idea was to exalt Lumumba as an otherworldly god with little contemporary relevance since Mobutu was said to be fulfilling all of Lumumba's political promises. But then a student got up and gave a long, fairly radical political speech that was vigorously applauded by all the students present. Afterward, a record was played of Lumumba delivering some of his strongly nationalist speeches. When President Joseph Kasavubu was then heard dismissing Lumumba, the prelude to Mobutu's first takeover, the students booed. Present at the meeting was Provincial Governor Bulundwe, a former supporter of the Katanga secession. He visibly squirmed in his seat.[4]

Nancy found teaching English at the Catholic girls' school tiring but rewarding. Her fifteen- to twenty-one-year-old high school students gave her more contact with local society than my university ones. They shared with her their traditional songs and recipes. Unlike the state-run high school where she had also worked, the students had books, their teachers generally taught subjects in which they were qualified, and the administration communicated high expectations and steady discipline. Still, she worried that most would eventually fail the state examinations for secondary school diplomas, foreclosing their entrance to advanced education and better jobs. Their previous education had been disrupted by Kisangani's rebellions and army mutinies, and instruction in science and mathematics was a weak point. A more fundamental problem was the rigid Belgian and French-style secondary school system, which was organized to credential only a narrow elite.

Living in the Congo also afforded me an opportunity to add details to my manuscript on U.S. policy in the early 1960s, which I hoped to publish. In Kisangani, I interviewed the former speaker of the National Assembly under Prime Minister Lumumba and the former chief of staff to Antoine Gizenga, Lumumba's deputy and political heir. The latter, one

Nancy and her English class at the Lycée Virgo Immaculata
in Kisangani

of my students, had accompanied Lumumba following his desperate escape from United Nations custody in Kinshasa to try to reach Stanleyville. He recounted how Lumumba was captured by Mobutu's troops only after insisting upon going back across a river to escort his wife to the opposite bank.

I found other interesting sources too. Benoît Verhaegen, a visiting professor from Lovanium University, was a Belgian political scientist who had authored the most detailed accounts of political events in the independent Congo. From his temporary base in the *Blocs*, Verhaegen, a hardy looking forty-year-old with a beard and shorts, would drive his Land Rover into the bush to interview former rural rebels. Declaring himself *"passioné"* by my thesis, he kindly offered to host my planned research trip to Kinshasa.

On Lovanium's impressive campus on the outskirts of the capital I exploited its library's collection of relevant newspapers and documents, discussed my work with Verhaegen's Belgian and Congolese colleagues, and journeyed to the city center to interview key U.S. officials and businessmen. The latter included the American ambassador, Sheldon Vance, who had previously played a role in State Department policy making, and the local representative of Maurice Tempelsman, an American diamond trader who was heavily invested in the Congo, close to Mobutu, and influential in the Democratic Party.

Benoît was an intriguing character. His writings were often critical of Congolese political elites and influenced by Marxist perspectives. He proudly told me that, as the chief of staff of a Congolese cabinet minister, he had been the only White man in the Lumumba government. He seemed like the kind of person the post-Lumumba regimes would *not* want to have around. Yet as a researcher, he continued to gain access to revealing official documents, including voluminous caches of records the military had seized from the rebels. Some of my colleagues suggested that he might be protected by someone in power, perhaps because of a favor he had done in the past. It was not until 2001 that I would learn, from an experts' report in the Belgian parliament's belated inquiry into Lumumba's death, that Verhaegen had been a major conduit for Belgian government funds designated for the overthrow of Lumumba's government.

Through Benoît, I was able to connect with the number two ranking official in the Belgian Embassy, the aforementioned Alfred Cahen. Alfred had been an "advisor" to Congolese Foreign Minister Justin Bomboko during much of the period I had studied. We agreed to meet during his planned future visit to Kisangani. A few months later, Monsieur Cahen was a bit surprised when a pretty young American woman—Nancy—knocked on his door at the luxurious Congo Palace Hotel to extend an invitation for lunch.

Over a repast served by Michel with oddly quivering hands—"to show respect" he later explained—Cahen confirmed the CIA's role in the overthrow of Lumumba, remarking that he knew Bomboko "had been paid" by the Agency at the time. Aside from the insights Alfred imparted on this and many other political events, Nancy and I came away from our conversation with an appreciation of his warmth and ironic humor. For a high-ranking diplomat—and I had interviewed dozens of them—he seemed unusually genuine.

~~~

CHAPTER 3

AN EAST AFRICAN ESCAPE
WITH A FATEFUL CONCLUSION

———

While our life in Kisangani was stimulating, it was somewhat hermetic. Unlike most of our neighbors, we lacked an automobile. Not that you could drive very far unless you were adventurous, given the decrepit state of the roads. Considering our delayed arrival, initial penury, and the several month delay in shipping vehicles from abroad (almost none were available in Kisangani), we had decided to use our slowly accumulating dollar savings (part of our salary was paid in dollars) for international travel in Africa and Europe. As the academic year ended, we looked forward to our summer vacation in East Africa. We did not anticipate that it would begin with an unexpected encounter with the remains of rural Belgian colonialism and end in a chance meeting with the ULC rector that would alter our trajectory at the university.

We got off to a challenging start. Having flown into the Eastern city of Goma, we had just missed the once-a-week taxi that would have taken us across the border to Uganda. However, we learned that if we took a small tourist bus that stopped at a town about a half an hour from the border, we might, albeit with some difficulty, get a taxi onward. We had absorbed enough of the enterprising spirit of people we knew in Kisangani—merchants who traveled long hours over terrible roads to gather produce, a young professor and his wife who had braved the crumbling network to visit the Pygmies—to take a chance rather than waste scarce time. The tourist bus dropped us off in the small town of Rutshuru as the sun was setting. On the main street we noticed only a large hotel and gas station.

Entering the hotel, I found the obviously drunk manager in the restaurant. He was yelling at a couple of women who may have been prostitutes. He casually tossed me a room key, gruffly letting me know there was no transportation to the border that day or the next. The hotel looked awfully empty. Nancy and I made a quick decision that this might not be the safest spot for our family—could we even trust the food?—and began to walk down the deserted street looking for an American mission hospital we had heard was in the area. As the sky darkened, we ran into a couple of friendly young men who took us to a different mission, with an adjoining church and school, run by the Belgian Catholic "White Fathers," named after the color of the robes they wore. After a while, one of the priests appeared, having returned from slaughtering a pig. He graciously offered us accommodation and a ride in the mission's Volkswagen to the border the next morning.

We spent a memorable evening with three slightly eccentric, elderly clerics. Over a light dinner, one of the men—who looked about eighty years old—showed off his perfectly accented English, chatted knowledgeably about World War

I, and referred to the Congolese in his outmoded colonial vocabulary as "natives." We felt we were drifting back in time. Another priest persisted in a vain effort to get Daniel to hold his pet cat, laughing all the while.

After dinner we were ushered into their living room, which contained a magnificent stereo system. It had been left behind, the men explained, by a Belgian settler who had fled during the unrest surrounding independence. A large cabinet was filled with records. I was offered an expensive looking cigar. The men displayed their collection of Congolese art, including many carved ivory pieces that they were quite willing to sell. Presently, they put on classical music and we all settled down to peruse recent Belgian magazines. Afterward, Nancy, Daniel, and I were led to our tiny room without running water or toilet. The moment we extinguished our lone light, the mission's generator was turned off, plunging the house and its environs into total darkness. Locating the outdoor toilet would be a challenge. Still, we were grateful for our glimpse into the life of an expiring colonial institution in rural Congo.

We were awakened at 5:30 a.m. by bells calling people to the church, which was as large as the Catholic cathedral in central Kisangani. After breakfast we compensated our hosts for their assistance and their driver took us to a hotel a mile across the Ugandan border. As the road ascended into the mountains, we passed herders with long staffs wearing shawls and coats in the cool morning air. As soon as we entered Uganda, we noticed that the people were better dressed than in Kisangani. Their houses looked firmer and had more protective tin roofs. There were more bicycles on the roads.

At the hotel, we arranged to hitchhike on a truck taking the manager to his doctor in the city of Kabale, from which we could find a commercial taxi to the capital, Kampala. Nancy and Daniel squeezed into the front cab while I attempted to sit on a borrowed hotel chair in the open back, a feat I mostly failed to accomplish on the rough road. For two hours we threaded our way through lovely mountains and clouds. Sometimes we saw houses that were enclosed in clouds.

Over the next month we flew and taxied (once with around fifteen people stuffed into three tiers of seats, another time with a group that brought along their goat) across Uganda, Kenya, and Tanzania. Sometimes the taxi driver left himself only half a seat. We loved exploring the large, diverse, and culturally sophisticated capitals of Kampala, Nairobi, and Dar es Salaam and touring the famous game parks in Tanzania.

In Kampala, a beautiful city rising on several hills, I gave a talk on my research at the distinguished, British-flavored Makerere University (afternoon tea was served). We luxuriated on such long-missed delicacies as ice cream and Indian and Chinese food. At sunset, we had drinks at an outdoor bar in "Bat Valley," a place where thousands of bats emerged from the adjoining forest, without once crashing into the fascinated customers. We found more modern, Western-looking central Nairobi less interesting though it featured some good shopping. One morning, I had a taxi take us to some of the outlying poor neighborhoods. The largest one was named "Lumumba."

In Moshi, Tanzania, we stayed at a hotel 3,000 feet up Mount Kilimanjaro and explored an adjoining banana plantation. Moving on to Arusha, beneath Mount Meru, we splurged on a tour of game parks via Land Rovers. In Lake Manyara, we marveled at the lions in trees and saw elephants, giraffes, impalas, and baboons. At Ngorongoro Crater, on the edge of the "Great Rift," we encountered traveling animal herds, including one of elephants that our driver/guide deftly maneuvered through. We picnicked while a jackal, large birds, and a few wildebeest waited nearby for the remains. At one point our driver excitedly sped off to a rare event that his trained eyes had discerned: two huge rhinoceri rhythmically mating for an extended time. On the spot, I shot my first and only erotic film.

In exotic Dar es Salaam, with its lovely mixture of European, Arab, Indian, and Swahili architecture, I gave a talk at the university, then an intellectual powerhouse of the African Left. We took in the evening breezes by the Indian Ocean alongside the city's substantial Indian community and splurged on a seaside hotel so we could swim in its warm waters.

Near the end of our sojourn in temperate, relatively mosquito-free East Africa, the Congo caught up with me. One morning in Dar, I wasn't feeling so well. While I rested, Nancy and Daniel took a long walk. Soon I was overtaken by chills and a high fever. Vainly, I ransacked our end-of- vacation, jumbled-up suitcase contents searching for a tiny bottle of malaria pills. At last Nancy returned with Daniel and called a local doctor who came to our hotel. He injected me with quinine, handed me a bottle of codeine pills, and to my astonishment, pronounced me sufficiently fit for our scheduled flight to Nairobi, Kenya, that same afternoon. I was embarrassingly high on codeine at the airport, laughing nonstop. But by the time we landed, my fever had begun to subside.

For our return to Kisangani, we first flew from Nairobi to Bujumbura, the capital of Burundi. There we overnighted at a hotel that was reputed to have hosted Chinese Communist operatives advising leaders of the 1960s rebellions. The manager kindly showed me their room.

At the hotel we unexpectedly ran into Ben Hobgood, the university's then (White) American missionary interim rector, and his family, who were also on vacation. Our brief conversation that evening would have a major impact on my future at the university and even my later professional life.

Over dinner—I remember Ben's daughters feasting on the Belgian French fries—I inquired whether we were going to be getting a new permanent rector as had been rumored. "Well Steve," he replied, "I've just written Professor [André] Lacocque about all the problems we have here. I honestly don't know whether he really wants to come and deal with them." Afterward, Nancy and I chatted about how unfortunate it was that Ben seemed to be conveying a discouraging picture of the university to his designated successor. We both wondered if he was possibly trying to hang on to his position.

Soon after our return to Kisangani, the university announced that Lacocque had unexpectedly rejected its offer of the rectorship on grounds of "health." I didn't know whether his decision had anything to do with Ben's letter, but I believed that the attitude Ben had conveyed *could* have been an obstacle to recruiting a new rector.

The next day we taxied past lovely Burundian hillside tea plantations to the Eastern Congo city of Bukavu. There we purchased two large baskets of the best ripe strawberries I have ever tasted and boarded the plane to Kisangani.

Back in our apartment, we felt refreshed. Daniel walked around for a while imitating giraffes munching leaves. But in the last months of 1970, things around the university began to change for us.

A few people with whom we had been friendly had departed at the end of the academic year, underlining the transience of our relationships. Moreover, it seemed that as the faculty continued to expand, its national groupings had reached a critical mass, where they could now become more exclusive. The Dutch went shopping with the Dutch; the French played bocce together; the Congolese with American wives hung out with each other. Western reporters and observers often comment on African "tribalism," which academics try to correct to "ethnicity" since traditional tribal structures have radically declined. Yet it was amazing to see how nationality-based cliques came to thrive among young, well-educated, non-African professionals living in an integrated residential setting.

Gradually, we began to feel more isolated. Nancy became somewhat depressed. She strongly missed her family and friends. She also longed for the cultural attractions of a large city, a feeling probably enhanced by our recent experience in East Africa. She spent more time listening to music cassettes that her mother sent her. In November she confided to her journal, which she shared with me only years later, that she was "living in a partial dream world, making up all kinds of ways to suddenly have to fly to New York: someone is sick, there's a Revolution."

Carried along by my work and characteristic optimism, I underplayed Nancy's distress, failed to detect her submerged anger. To my regret, I remember asking her why she couldn't handle the situation as well as other young women at the university we knew.

At the same time, my own circumstances were changing. I would soon feel compelled to make a series of difficult choices. These emerged, beginning in December, as Congolese students, faculty, and mid-level administrative staff began to move, a decade after independence, to "decolonize" the university. The consequences of my decisions during that month would help place our family in a vulnerable position when the university erupted for a second time in March 1971. Then the student boycott and government clampdown would supply the final ingredients for a "perfect storm," one that would allow Nancy's fantasy of escape to come true.

~

CHAPTER 4

TAKING RISKS, I

I*t all began in December 1970*, one year after our arrival. Acting through their government-mandated, single political party organizations, the Congolese students, faculty, and administrative staff dispatched memoranda to the university's board of trustees urging the ouster of Interim Rector Hobgood. They demanded that he be temporarily replaced by Congolese Vice-Rector for Student Affairs Koli while a permanent Congolese rector with a doctorate was recruited.

Koli had earned his master's degree in political science from Wayne State University in Detroit. As previously noted, he had recently been elected to President Mobutu's parliament and modeled himself on the Congo's "Big Man." Like his hero and patron who was promoting African "authenticity," he sported the open-necked *abacost* (a light, buttoned, collarless suit, worn without a shirt and tie). The name of this outfit was a clever abbreviation of the French phrase *à bas le costume*, which means "Down with the [Western] suit."

Convinced that graduation from the university was their only route out of poverty, the students held Hobgood, not their own government, accountable for conditions they saw blocking their ascent. These included poor housing and restaurant facilities, professors teaching courses outside of their qualifications, a dearth of mentors for Congolese teaching assistants, and a high student failure rate. They asserted that Hobgood's designated, highly regarded successor, the Belgian-born, Chicago Theological Seminary Professor André Lacocque, had withdrawn primarily because of "a struggle for influence" among "certain groups" in the university's leadership that were themselves trying to "conquer the Rectorship."

The Congolese professors and staff were also critical of Lacocque's demise, which they similarly attributed to "bad spirit and maneuvering" in the administration (reference was made to a struggle between Americans and Dutch for "hegemony"). Further, they alleged racial discrimination in recruitment and promotion. Among teaching applicants with equal qualifications, they added, Congolese should receive preference.

As most of the Congolese professors were still pursuing their terminal graduate degrees, they thought that the university should provide them with increased mentoring, research assistance, and course load reductions. Unhappy that White deans headed six of the university's seven "Faculties" (equivalent to American universities' "Schools"), they maintained that as Congolese with relevant doctorates became available, all deans should be nationals. They bitterly denounced a "crisis of Negrophobia or a mania for detesting Blacks and distrusting them," insisting that the foreigner's role at the university was to help the Congolese, not direct them.

In my eyes, Ben Hobgood, a trim, slightly balding middle-aged man, was a serious, even-tempered Disciples of Christ Missionary. His cordial wife, Betsy, was the head of the university's financially starved library, and they had three spunky daughters. Ben was clearly devoted to the Congo, where he had grown up in a missionary family and spent most of his forty-two years. As a child, he had traveled through the hinterland with his father, a peripatetic rural evangelist. After spending his college years in Kentucky, he returned to the Congo during the last years of colonial rule, serving as the pastor of a large urban church, then being tasked to assist in the formation of a Protestant-inspired university. Ben's fundraising efforts in the United States, including with the U.S. Agency for International Development (USAID), and his sheer perseverance had been crucial to the young university's survival. Undoubtedly, some of the material shortcomings and construction delays for which he was blamed were mainly attributable to the Congolese government.

Still, Ben, who held a bachelor's degree in divinity studies, seemed surpassed by the administrative and academic requirements of leading one of post-independence Congo's three universities. For one thing, the institution was so over-centralized that the smallest decisions were interminably delayed. Its "executive council" had to meet to approve a change in the price of photocopying.

As a result of these circumstances, I learned that lower-level administrators frequently ploughed ahead with unapproved side deals that derailed the budget. Some of my colleagues, as well as the American Consul, thought the administration's authoritarian bent stemmed from foreign missionaries' outdated distrust of their Congolese subalterns. Galen Hull, a young American who taught English, later wrote, "The administration assumed that a Congolese would embezzle until he managed to prove himself innocent."[5] Certainly, Ben projected a personal image of control with a heavy set of keys dangling from his waist, a practice imitated by the university's top Congolese administrators.

Most disturbing to me, the administration he headed didn't seem to have the slightest idea of how to improve the educational success of its ambitious students—half of whom were projected to fail—and made no effort to adjust Western academic curricula to the needs of a young African state.

Furthermore, Ben was out of sync with his Congolese constituents' aspirations to exert major influence over "their" institution. His racial perspectives were, to say the least, anachronistic. Once, in my and Nancy's presence, he lamented Africans' inability to think abstractly and their consequent lack of aptitude for mathematics. On another occasion, he assured me that my sometimes ill Congolese students didn't need malaria pills because they had developed a "natural immunity" to the disease—a gross medical exaggeration. (According to the Severe Malaria Observatory, as late as 2020 there were an estimated 30 million cases of malaria in the Congo, the second highest number globally.)

As the board of trustees convened, the new, racially fraught conflict on our previously quiet campus heated up. The entire student body went out on strike. Five of the six White deans wrote the trustees expressing their "profound distress" at the Congolese demands, which, they maintained, threatened to undermine foreign fundraising and personnel recruitment and damage the quality of education. They requested that the board clarify "whether there is still a place for qualified foreigners at our university" by formally disassociating itself from the Congolese memoranda. Seeming to underline the point, the American dean of natural sciences—whose surname was ironically Stanley—tendered his resignation. This triggered an angry riposte from the Congolese faculty/staff organization denouncing Stanley's move as "racial, chauvinist . . . blackmail."

As tensions rose, the administration furnished almost no information to the university community, I learned about the Congolese student, faculty, and staff demands belatedly from the local Kisangani newspaper and a Congolese colleague. News of the deans' letter and Stanley's resignation reached me through my friend Alistair, who was secretary of the theology faculty. Arriving on campus to find no students in their classrooms, the professors simply assumed they were on vacation until further notice! Nothing better illustrated the absence of real community at the university.

With classes suspended and reliable information lacking, the political scientist in me was curious to know more about my students' grievances. One morning, I happened to be at the administration building picking up my mail. As I emerged, a student leaned out of the window of a parked university bus and lightly suggested I join them. I thought to myself, "Why not? Maybe I can learn something about what's happening." Since I was supervising my students' research, why not do a little of my own? I boarded the bus, although I had no idea where it was going. As we departed, a student joked, to good-humored laughter, "We've captured a missionary."

Within several minutes we arrived at the "Sabena Guest House" opposite the airport. The university had turned a former Belgian airline hotel into its main dormitory for unmarried students. As many as four students shared a single room. Descending from the bus, I found myself enveloped in a slow-moving crowd. Stalled for a few moments, I picked up an interesting looking vine from the ground. For a guy from Queens, Kisangani was a botanical wonderland with its stunning variety of plants and brightly colored flowers.

As the crowd carried me forward, I almost collided with a mock wooden coffin for Rector Hobgood. "Rest in Peace" read the markings on top. Almost instinctively, but with a sense of doing something humorous, I dropped my vine onto it, provoking a cheer from some of the students. I was at first bemused—but quickly discomfited—by this unexpected turn of events, which I realized associated me with the students' demonstration.

Seeing no prospect for meaningful discussion in this environment, I headed across the street to the airport and began to think about how I would get back to the university. When I reached the other side, I turned around to notice a young, black-bearded White man I had never seen before taking my picture. As he disappeared into the crowd, I thought to myself, "Uh oh, I don't think he's just a tourist. Maybe the government or one of its foreign government supporters is spying on the students." Then, with my characteristic rationalism and optimism, I tried to minimize any potential consequences for myself. All I had really done, I thought/rationalized, was to spontaneously throw a vine on a mock coffin I accidentally happened upon in front of the dormitory.

A day or two later I had a less casual, and much more questionable, encounter.

Again retrieving my mail, I happened to run into one
of my best students. Still thirsting to understand what was
happening, I asked him for his take.

During our long, informative discussion of the students'
perspective and actions, he referred specifically to their belief
that Hobgood had "discouraged" Lacocque, his putative successor. My thoughts immediately turned to the letter Hobgood
had told Nancy and me about three months earlier, in which
he had warned Lacocque of the "difficulties" he would face if
he accepted the rector position. It tended to support, though
did not prove, the students' conviction.

After a too brief internal debate, I decided to recount our
conversation with Hobgood and my reaction to it, expecting
that my student would probably share it with others. I was
aware that I was taking a risk. If I were identified as the source
of the information, it would damage my relationship with the
Hobgoods and their missionary and other supporters. That
was why I asked the student to keep my name and national-
ity confidential. Although he agreed, I realized he might not
comply given our purely classroom relationship and the stakes
involved in the protest. And I knew that even if my report
got out without attribution, the Hobgoods might guess that
I was the source.

Why on earth, then, did I take the chance of offending
the university's besieged rector and his allies when I had come
to the Congo purely to teach and learn? I remember being
motivated by my general sympathy for the students' struggle and demands and my desire to equalize my transaction
with my student. Here I was plumbing him for numerous
details concerning the student movement. Why should I in

turn withhold relevant information he and his colleagues surely deserved to know? At a more emotional level, I only half-sensed my yearning to overcome my feelings of isolation from the students I had been teaching. After a year on a campus where faculty and students led segregated lives, where teachers had no places to receive students and the few student publications were not generally distributed, I grasped at an opportunity to forge a modest connection to my students' aspirations. As I think about it, that was also one of the reasons why I jumped on that bus. In retrospect, I should have more fully recognized this emotional impulse and subjected it to scrutiny.

Instead, I rationalized: "What's wrong with my sharing relevant information with the students who are conducting a well-organized, peaceful campaign for a better university?" I wasn't participating in or organizing their actions. Furthermore, unlike the bloody Lovanium University protests in the capital eighteen months earlier, the students here were neither challenging the political regime nor doing so in its heartland. To the contrary, there was good reason to believe that the government, through its single-party Congolese student, faculty, and staff organizations that were calling for the rector's departure and Mobutu-favorite Koli's elevation, was itself complicit in the anti-Hobgood movement.

Sure, I was taking the risk of antagonizing the rector and his supporters. But the majority of professors Nancy and I socialized with gossiped frequently about the failures of the university administration. I wasn't alone. Yes, I had taken it up a notch by sharing relevant information with striking students. Still, I thought I could live with any potential negative reactions from the Hobgood camp. Anyway, I had only seven months to go in my teaching contract.

A day or two after I imparted my information, the trustees gathered at a house off campus. During the evening, the residence was besieged by a large group of students. Some threw rocks, breaking windows and inflicting minor cuts. The house's phone lines were reportedly cut and at least one car was set afire. For unknown reasons, nearby police failed to show up.

Under these intimidating conditions the board, which for its own reasons had reportedly been considering replacing Hobgood in the near future, caved. It decided to accept Hobgood's immediate resignation, appoint Koli interim rector, and search for a permanent rector who would be Congolese, Protestant, and hold a doctorate. The Mobutu government quickly confirmed the trustees' decisions (although Ben told me at his farewell party that he had rejected an offer by Mobutu to send troops to maintain him in office). There was no effort by the new university leadership or government to punish the students for their boycott of classes or night of mini revolution.

While I was generally relieved by these results, I was uneasy when I learned about the minor violence outside the trustees' meeting. Encountering the student in whom I had confided, I asked, "Do you think the information I gave you played any role in those climactic events?" After pondering a few seconds, he answered, "We all believed that Hobgood had discouraged his successor. Now we had proof."

That disturbed me. I had offered some evidence for that conclusion but had also made clear it was far from proof. Still,

I should have anticipated that in the inflamed, racially charged atmosphere, it could have looked like proof. Although my act of information-sharing was only a minor piece of what was happening, I didn't like being left with the impression that it might have contributed to the violence during the protest.

Furthermore, despite the warning signs of the White deans' letter and Professor Stanley's resignation, I had underestimated the price Nancy and I might pay for my actions with the more conservative elements of the White expatriate community.

Ben's fate shocked many of his fellow American missionaries and their families—and not just because many had close personal relationships with him. They lamented the Congolese's "lack of gratitude" for their longtime contributions to "development." On the other side, Congolese felt that an emphasis on these contributions, which they could never repay, locked them into a neocolonial system of continued foreign domination.[6] In addition, the minority of foreign professors and administrators who intended to stay longer than two years was shaken by the Congolese demands for rapid Africanization of employment and the accompanying nationalist rhetoric. This was especially the case for less qualified foreign staff.

Lastly, many Whites tended to view the crisis through a zero-sum racial lens. They misperceived the Congolese as wanting to eject all Whites, even though, in condemning Stanley's resignation, the Congolese faculty and staff had proclaimed their "sympathy for all foreigners of good will."

In this emotionally overheated environment, exaggerated, even false, reports of my alleged contribution to Hobgood's demise spread among American missionaries and others sympathetic to the deposed rector.

"Y" was a young woman who had recently arrived to take up a job as a secretary in the administration. In her spare time, she had volunteered to help type my thesis revisions. She struck me as a quiet, conscientious, agreeable person. But now she sent me an angry, sarcastic note chastising me for "kneeling at Hobgood's grave." In the future, Y suggested, she might send me photocopies of important official letters to prevent me from telling "untrue stories" that discouraged foreign donors. She further advised that if I wanted Congolese students to replace a Protestant rector with a Muslim, Jew, or atheist, I should urge Hebrew University in Jerusalem to replace theirs with a Catholic or Protestant. While Nancy was convinced that this last, baseless remark was anti-Semitic, I put it down to Y's misinformation about the Congolese demands.

Interestingly, I later learned that Lacocque, the Protestant theologian who was Hobgood's putative successor, held a doctorate in Jewish literature and had founded a Center for Jewish and Christian Studies at his seminary. During World War II his Belgian family had sheltered Jews from the Nazi occupation and his father subsequently converted to Judaism and emigrated to Israel.

Finally, I had never even considered the possibility that pumped up versions of my actions might reach—and be given credence by—the Congo's cabinet and the American Embassy in Kinshasa. Two weeks after the events, U.S. Ambassador Sheldon Vance met with the Congo's minister of the interior, our former provincial governor, Edouard Bulundwe, who had flown to Kisangani to investigate Hobgood's dethroning. Forty-three years later, I discovered, in the U.S. National Archives, the embassy's January 2, 1971, report of their discussion.[7] After reassuring Vance that the causes of the student demonstration at the USAID-supported institution were due to "specific problems of the university and not to any anti-American bias," Bulundwe observed:

> . . . that his investigations had indicated that there was an "anti-American American" named Weis[s]man on the faculty who had been one of the principal agitators in this affair. He thought that Weis[s]man for reasons of his own had been working surreptitiously for some time to undermine Hobgood and foreigners in general in the university.

From this paranoid picture of my motives and the comment by the ambassador noted below, it is pretty obvious that a major source of the government's information was the pro-Hobgood camp. Significantly, the minister did not indicate that his government felt strongly enough about the matter to take any action against me for my alleged agitation.

At the end of his report of his report Vance stated:

> We have heard from several sources, including members of the University Administration, that Weis[s]man was an active participant in the student demonstration during the meeting of the Council on the night of December 16–17.

Despite his claimed multiplicity of sources, the ambassador was sending Washington false information. I had not been present at the demonstration. I was so isolated from the students' actions I didn't even know that the trustees were meeting that night. The chief U.S. representative in Kisangani, Consul Bob Strand, would have learned that had he bothered to consult me. Strand later cabled the State Department that I had spread "what proved later to be a false and irresponsible, if not malicious report" that Hobgood "had scared off Lacocque with a letter giving a dismal picture of the problems of running the university."[8] Yet I had only repeated what Hobgood himself had told me and had not gone as far as claiming the letter had "scared off" the candidate.

In retrospect, the crescendoing costs of my risk-taking clearly outweighed the benefits. I would have been better off staying completely away from the students during the December protests. Knowing I was at a university where there was a lack of authentic communication and trust between the university's racial communities, I should have better anticipated how people on both sides of the developing racially charged conflict might perceive, misinterpret, and react to my expressions. Indeed, through my scholarly research I was well versed in the volatility of Black-White relations in post-independence Congo, including the spread of poisonous rumors of racial violence. Yet despite my academic knowledge, my "gut" reactions to the fast-breaking events around me failed to adequately consider their potential explosiveness.

At the same time, given the absence of community and the information vacuum surrounding me, it would have been difficult for me to *fully* imagine the breadth and intensity of the scenario that had unfolded: the unprecedented militancy of the previously disciplined student demonstrators, the public explosion of strong feelings of racial alienation and national humiliation from formerly quiescent Congolese professors and administrators, the profound sense of betrayal felt by the missionaries and other conservative Whites as well as their fears of displacement, and the uncontrolled spread of misinformation about my conduct within the secretive Congolese and American governments. Writing about these racial and political dynamics more than fifty years later, I cannot help but think about contemporary American parallels in the aftermath of the 2020 murder of George Floyd.

~~

CHAPTER 5

TAKING RISKS, II

I *confess to making two more* debatable choices in the
following weeks, ones that probably also contributed
to my ultimate downfall. Here is where my story becomes, at
least in retrospect, rather comic.

In January 1971, a month after the crisis, a Spanish political scientist named Luis Beltran was elected dean of our
economic and social sciences faculty. Just before the election,
I was approached by two Congolese professors, one educated
in America, the other in the Soviet Union, who urged me
to run against him. They explained that the few Congolese
professors in our faculty wanted someone in that position who
was sympathetic to their nationalist aspirations. The Congolese
themselves could not run because they had not yet completed
their doctorates. I was given to understand that it wasn't necessary for me to campaign; they would organize my support.
Although I had no desire to get into academic administration
in my last months at the university, I was flattered by their
confidence and agreed they could nominate me.

During the election meeting, neither candidate was called
upon to speak about their qualifications and plans. When
the vote transpired, I got thumped, 14 to 7. It appeared that

professors who identified more with "Europe," including a couple of Congolese ones, voted for the Spaniard, while those more oriented to the U.S. voted for the American. I got over my defeat in a couple of weeks, but Dean Beltran seemed to cool toward me.

Soon afterward, I was required to comment at a student's public defense of his senior thesis. His subject was an analysis of the provincial administration's revenues. Called in late to be his second reader, I had helped him complete his *memoire* in the face of continuing, non-substantive criticisms of its grammar and form by his primary reviewer, who had also been recently assigned.

I began my remarks by observing that the author had worked hard and produced an acceptable study despite being hampered by repeated changes of his thesis director. I went on to mention a few weaknesses in his analysis, making the point that these demonstrated the need for additional faculty mentors who themselves conducted research on African public administration. For example, the thesis assumed that it was as easy to tax small traders in Kisangani as in Paris, which was certainly not the case.

In planning my comments, I had been concerned that, however delicately and impersonally they were phrased, they would come off as a criticism of the thesis's current director, Professor Tung, a congenial colleague from South Vietnam. Nevertheless, I decided that it was unfair to burden the student alone with my reservations. Whoever showed up at this educational event deserved to be informed of the fundamental weakness of the university's overly Westernized social science instruction. I was probably also influenced by the rising tide of Congolese nationalism that had just propelled Koli to the University's helm. Since I was unaware of any norm restricting my remarks, I spoke from my heart. When I finished, the audience—unexpectedly large and overwhelmingly students—erupted in prolonged applause.

To my relief, Professor Tung evinced a remarkable ability to go with, and even surpass, the flow. He said that he *agreed* with my comments, further explaining, as a student newsletter later reported, that he "hadn't had time to read, reread and analyze the principal ideas of the [thesis]."

Nevertheless, at our February faculty meeting, Professor David, a sharp Indian economist sitting next to Tung, complained, pithily, that my intervention at the defense had been "*peu catholique,*" i.e., not very generous. I couldn't help but notice that he smelled strongly of whiskey. Dean Beltran, with his wavy black hair and expressive face, commented that he had read the transcript of the session and I had been "saying some things that were out of place, perhaps with the intention of having yourself applauded." Within minutes of this rather ungracious remark, he progressed to blaming me for a slowly developing student boycott of Professor G's political economy course, of which I had been unaware.

It turned out that both the students concerned and the vice-rector for student affairs had suggested that dissatisfaction with Professor G was linked to a gap between the Initiation to Economics course the students had taken during their freshman year and his sophomore year offering.

However, Dean Beltran had a whole other idea. The problem, he said, was that Professor Weissman's History of Political Thought course "talked only about Aristotle, Machiavelli,

Marx, Mao, etc." and therefore had "nothing economic" in it. No wonder, he concluded, G's students were unable to apprehend his teaching. Two of my colleagues jumped up to point out that there was not supposed to be any juncture between my political science course and G's economics one, and to boot the two courses were being taught simultaneously. If Dean Beltran perceived a problem with my course, one advised, he should have approached me privately rather than attack me publicly. "With the atmosphere of the meeting becoming a little tense," our faculty secretary recorded: "The Dean adjourned the meeting without discussing the miscellaneous items.

Beltran invited me to drop by his office the following day. I had been shocked by his assault. He had always seemed to me an interesting, if somewhat distant, guy. He had a charming Irish wife, a cute son about Daniel's age, a wonderful old blue and white Chevrolet convertible, and a formidable home library from which I had once borrowed a book. Was he angry at me for running, however unsuccessfully, for the deanship? Was he perhaps manifesting a lack of sympathy for someone whom he associated with the Congolese professors' nationalist demands that could eventually cost him his job? Maybe, I thought, he was just a little weird—like several other members of our heterogeneous community. With my usual rationalism and optimism, I hoped that our forthcoming chat would help us get past the strain in our relationship.

It was not to be. Beltran began our meeting by informing me that in my remaining semester I would carry a course load that I knew to be about 50 percent heavier than those of our colleagues. Dismissing my reasoned objections to this inequity, he steadfastly refused to offer any justification for his decision. Then he began to berate me for giving out too many As to my students and not failing more of them. American or U.S.-educated Congolese professors in our faculty generally graded higher than their European-trained colleagues. The dean made no concession to my defense of my grading system, which was the same as I had used at Fordham.

As we argued back and forth, the moment arrived when my threshold for humiliation was exceeded, and my internal controls collapsed. Formulating my words slowly, I asked, "Do you know what you are, Monsieur Beltran?" "No, what am I?" he replied matter-of-factly. "*Vous êtes un stupide,*" (You're a stupid guy) I cried, plunging in my dagger. "*Vous êtes un stupide,*" he answered, rather unimaginatively.

Ridiculously, each of us repeated our denunciations as he flung open the door to the anteroom, where his secretary sat. Rushing past me, he bolted out of the front door of the Six Codo, leapt into his cool convertible, and sped off under the midday sun toward the administration building, trailing a large flurry of brown dust. Upon his arrival, I later learned, he complained to the vice-rector of academic affairs that I had insulted him in front of his secretary and within the hearing of a few students nearby.

I admit that in the United States it is not appropriate to insult your dean, even with provocation. But in Kisangani my violation of this norm would be accompanied by particularly heavy consequences.

A week later, every professor at the university received a stern, almost farcical communiqué from Interim Rector Koli, which read in part:

It has come back to me that certain professors, oblivious to their role as educators, are devoting their most precious leisure time to giving their students model lessons in hateful and insulting talk and spiteful pugilism.

This movement is at such a rhythm that it is thrusting its outrageous temerity to reach the persons of academic authorities, victims of their duties.

This university is not a nursery for scholars without morality, but a garden bringing together and cultivating all the virtues of mankind which aspires to perfection.

That is why I will not hesitate to apply the necessary regulatory measures to our professors who continue to abuse our confidence and do not show they have changed their ways.

I had the sinking feeling that I might be one of the offenders Koli had in mind, possibly the only one. Considering myself duly warned, I put my head down and scrupulously avoided Dean Beltran.

But it was too late. My post-Hobgood chickens came home to roost in late March when the new, insecure university administration headed by Koli and Vice-Rector A proved unable to end the expanding, increasingly militant student boycott, and the provincial and national governments became alarmed. By pinning part of the blame for the morass on me and my alleged Maoist teachings—even though I had nothing to do with the latest protest—the university administration achieved two objectives: It struck back at an irritant who had displeased it in several ways and offered the government a convenient scapegoat for the latest crisis, an American of whom it was already suspicious from the Hobgood imbroglio.

Looking backward, I am somewhat less critical of my behavior after Hobgood's cashiering than before. Yes, I could have been more patient with Beltran's humiliations, maybe just walked out of his office. And I might have submerged my educational concerns at the thesis defense. On the other hand, I had no reason to think that my expressions would be so damaging to me. And, crucially, my choices would not have been so consequential had there not been the sudden new crisis unleashed by the boycott of Professor G's class. Absent that unexpected development, I would have almost certainly been able to complete my teaching contract in July.

It quickly became apparent that much of the initiative for my removal had come from the university authorities, with the nervous government, already wary of me, mainly ratifying their analysis. The day after we flew to Kinshasa, the professors was assembled for what our friend Mary wrote us was "an intimidation session." The two vice-ministers laid out my sins: teaching a course on Maoism, criticizing other professors in front of students, and "demagoguery." The latter two accusations clearly derived from the administration's disquiet over my confrontation with Beltran and performance at the thesis defense. As for my alleged Maoist agitation, Rector Koli subsequently admitted to Alistair and Mary that he had helped finger me to the government. When the already suspicious Presidential Intelligence Bureau requested a copy of my political theory course, he sent it only the undistributed, mimeographed copy of a Mao excerpt just produced by the printer. "Naturally,"

Koli lamely explained to my friends, "I gave them the only thing I had."

Both the faculty "intimidation session" and subsequent national developments also revealed that the action taken against the alleged student ringleaders and me was part of a broader crackdown on universities being jointly undertaken by the government and university administration. Thus, the vice-ministers instructed the professors how to dress and warned that they ought not to be critical of the Congo.

The university leaders' political and personal insecurities were on full display. Earlier, the rector had laid bare some of his anxieties in a series of communiqués accusing unnamed administrative and academic officials of "inadmissible carelessness" and a "depraved" lack of discipline. He had also vaunted the university's "generous" contribution to President Mobutu's success in winning 100 percent of the province's votes for his unopposed re-election. Despite having risen to power through a kind of democratic anti-colonial mini revolution, Koli now proceeded to warn the professors, "*Je suis dictateur* (I am the dictator)," cautioning them, "There are [government] spies everywhere."

In the following days, the ULC's search for enemies assumed Kafkaesque proportions. Vice-Rector A opined that it had been necessary to discipline the student boycotters because they were involved in "tribalist" plots to replace Koli. The latter announced that he possessed "a drawer full of letters written to foreign addresses by foreign professors criticizing the government or the university" and that he was "was planning to confront these professors with their crimes."

Regarding the faculty's reactions to these pronouncements, Mary wrote, "The fear and paranoia were so absurdly intense that we all had to bite our cheeks to keep from laughing . . . obviously they are out to rule by creating fear, and that is a bit of a joke since it is they who are more afraid than we!"

Following a week of suspended classes, the university reopened, minus about two dozen students who had been expelled. According to my former students, those punished were mainly individuals listed on the mastheads of two student newsletters that had run stories criticizing Professor G. After a year of struggling to support themselves and their families, they were permitted to re-enroll. Friends also wrote that politically suspect faculty were being purged. A professor from Mauritius, in East Africa, was fired and a couple of Congolese professors were told their contracts would not be renewed. At least two American professors indicated they would not return as expected for the next academic year.

It was not long before it became clear that the government's crackdown on universities went beyond Kisangani. Two months after our departure in early April, students at Lovanium organized a street demonstration in Kinshasa in memory of those killed by government troops in 1969. There is no evidence that they were inspired by the events in Kisangani. After the memorial was brutally suppressed, the government closed the school and enrolled the entire student body in the army. The authorities then decided to merge the three universities into a single, now fully state-controlled institution, redistributing faculties and departments across three different campuses. My students ended up being split between Kinshasa and Lubumbashi.

In retrospect, the turbulent events I lived through in Kisangani represented an important moment of political transition, one in which the authoritarian Congolese government was moving to exert greater single-party control of all major civil society groups, especially youth and student associations, trade unions, and religious organizations. This was part of a widespread trend in Sub-Saharan Africa. In the Congo, it would morph into a broader state expansion under Mobutu from 1970 to 1974, which established, as leading scholars of the country later noted, "an astonishing personal hegemony."[9]

When I revisit these long-ago experiences, I realize that I was making choices in a rapidly changing political environment in a country far different from my own. My university had unexpectedly plunged into an intense post-colonial struggle between a Black African majority and a conservative White expatriate minority, one which I was not fully prepared to appreciate despite my extensive academic studies.

Despite a patina of academic freedom, the norms for faculty conduct, including which violations might be severely sanctioned, were largely unwritten and unclear. With a dearth of authentic communication among the diverse elements of the university and my ignorance of government and U.S. Embassy thinking, it was difficult for me to fully estimate the potential consequences of my actions. In the absence of long-term friends, experienced and trusted colleagues, or family members, there was no one I felt comfortable calling upon for sage advice. Hence, at times I imprudently allowed my values and sympathies to roam relatively freely.

To further complicate my decision-making, under the surface, the single political party structure and the university were undergoing a quiet transition toward greater top-down control by the Mobutu regime. It was not easy for me to see where power lay. The government had appeared to support the overthrow of the old American missionary-led "neocolonial" order by its single-party student, faculty, and administrative organizations. Yet, as I discovered only decades later, it was also concerned about my alleged "anti-American" role in helping provoke student unrest. When a second student strike emerged, it decided to crack down on some of those who had made or sympathized with the earlier mini revolution.

With the benefit of five decades of hindsight, I am struck by how much the exotic illuminated the commonplace. That is one reason those events continue to resonate with me. Back home in the United States, in more familiar and stable circumstances, I would confront, year after year, the same basic question I faced in Kisangani. Should I, in this professional situation, take a risk to try and advance my values or are the costs likely to outweigh the benefits?

Although I would find clearer standards for appropriate behavior in the U.S. as a university professor, foundation program officer, congressional staffer, administration advisor, and public policy researcher and advocate, the rules were sometimes contradictory or difficult to apply. And while the potential consequences of my contemplated actions were easier to foresee, there was often some ambiguity there as well. As in the Congo, my choice was usually not about *doing* something but *saying* something. Should I disagree with a superior, however respectfully? Should I ask an important question that might prove unwelcome to someone who does not share my views? How should I handle unjustified private and public attacks upon my judgment?

In both places, I faced the challenge of finding the sweet spot between recklessly affirming my values and judgments and cravenly withdrawing into my shell. In its starkness and surrealism, my experience as a young man in Kisangani more fully exposed who I really was and the path I would have to navigate in the future.

~~~

CHAPTER 6

JUDGMENT DAYS

W*e had arrived in Kinshasa* on Sunday evening under the injunction that I report to the interior minister. Monday morning, I telephoned the American Embassy. I knew from my research that the U.S. government had played a major role in President Mobutu's ascent to power a few years earlier and that no other country—not even the former colonial power, Belgium—had as much political clout with him. I had no idea that the embassy held a significantly inaccurate, extremely critical view of my actions in the Hobgood affair. I believed that my government would try to help me once it heard my story and saw how ridiculous the principal, "Maoist agitator" charge was.

Despite my "possible arrest situation" message, which had been forwarded to Kinshasa by the consulate, the embassy staff with whom I spoke seemed unaware of, then unconcerned by, my plight. Only after my anxious persistence did they finally agree to arrange a meeting with Ambassador Vance.

Later that day I sat in a conference room with the ambassador, an amazingly tall, distinguished, gray-haired gentleman, and his staff. We had met several months earlier when I had interviewed him for my book on past U.S. Congo policy. The first thing he said to me was that my expulsion from Kisangani had come as "a complete surprise." He invited me to inform him about what had happened.

I launched into an impassioned discussion of the latest events, the injustice of the allegations against me, and the reasons why I might have been singled out for punishment. Regarding the latter, I brought up the impact of my earlier sympathy for the movement against Hobgood, but prudently left out my conversation with my student about Hobgood's letter to Lacocque, fearing it would reinforce the false charge that I had incited the students against Professor G. Sitting back, I wondered whether I had gotten through to the imperturbable figure looming before me.

The ambassador evinced no reaction. He did not ask me any questions. Nor did he offer to send a U.S. official with me to see the minister of the interior. Only after I repeatedly emphasized how important it was for me, an American citizen threatened with arrest, to be accompanied by a representative of my government, did he finally agree to designate a staff member who would also set up my appointment. This is how I clearly remember it. There is, regrettably, no record of our meeting in the State Department records at the National Archives.

I was pretty good at denial, but the strain was beginning to show. That night I stood in the hallway of the Mission Guest House gazing at Nancy and Daniel and breaking down in tears. Nancy said it was the first time she had seen me cry in the five years we had loved each other.

The next day, Minister of Interior Bulundwe, a large man, ushered us into his office. I had met him while he was provincial governor, at the fancy outdoor reception at his luxurious villa in Kisangani. After staring at me for a few seconds, he inquired, somewhat irritably, "Why are you here?" I responded that his vice-minister had ordered me to leave Kisangani and report to him. Bulundwe then turned toward my accompanying American diplomat. "I don't understand," he said, "President Mobutu spoke to the ambassador about this a few days ago." The embassy officer sat silent and expressionless.

Bulundwe then reached into a file and handed me a mimeographed copy of the fifteen pages of excerpts from Mao's writings that I had deposited at the university printer's office. One of Mao's essays had the most unfortunate title, "A Single Spark Can Cause a Prairie Fire." The minister said he had been told that I had handed it out to the boycotting students. After I explained to him the truth of the matter, he commented, "You are not charged with anything. I am waiting for the final report from the vice-minister and others sent to investigate the situation in Kisangani. We've just removed you from the situation."

Only slightly relieved, I pursued, "But today's main Kinshasa newspaper says that the two vice-ministers "recognized" that I was "guilty of inciting the students to insubordination," and this week's *Zaire* magazine says that I "incited" the students "to the point of committing assaults on the academic authorities."

Bulundwe abruptly wheeled around in his chair and pulled out a shelf behind him that contained some kind of radio transmitter. "Get me the vice-minister in Kisangani," he barked into the microphone. When the latter came on, the minister had just four words for him: "No more press conferences!" he shouted. Well, that was more encouraging, I thought. The minister then informed me that, for now, I was free to go anywhere in the Congo—except Kisangani.

As we were leaving, Bulundwe pulled me aside and posed a stunning question: "Why did your wife refuse to shake hands with the vice-rector for academic affairs at the airport?" For a moment, his query brought home to me the absurdity of our situation. Then my heart filled with pride as I explained to the minister Nancy's quiet act of conscience, which had apparently resonated with Vice-Rector A and others.

As we departed, I casually asked the embassy officer, "Do you know why the ambassador didn't mention yesterday that he had discussed my case with President Mobutu"? He shrugged his shoulders.

More than four decades later, I discovered a March 27, 1971, embassy cable in the National Archives reporting to Washington on a conversation between Ambassador Vance and President Mobutu the day before my firing.[10] Mobutu had told the ambassador that he had decided to close the university pending a "thorough investigation" of faculty and students responsible for recent demonstrations, including a "physical attack" on acting Rector Koli who was also a member of Parliament. (According to a news story, a student had spit on him.) Vowing that "guilty faculty members and students would not be continued," Mobutu said, "several members of the faculty had been fomenting trouble in the student body dating back to the troubles that had led to the dismissal of former Rector Hobgood."

One of these, he related, "is an American named Weissman he is informed had been teaching Maoism and other subversive doctrines in his political science classes." Nothing in the cable indicated that the ambassador provided any response to Mobutu's statements.

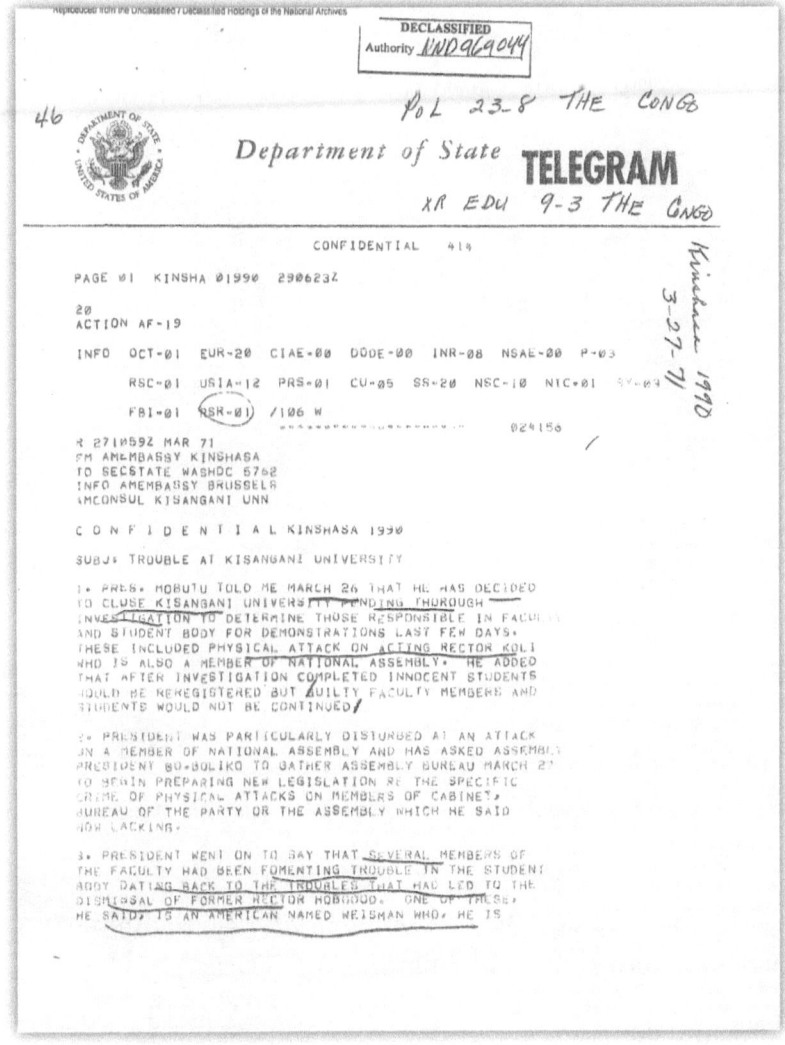

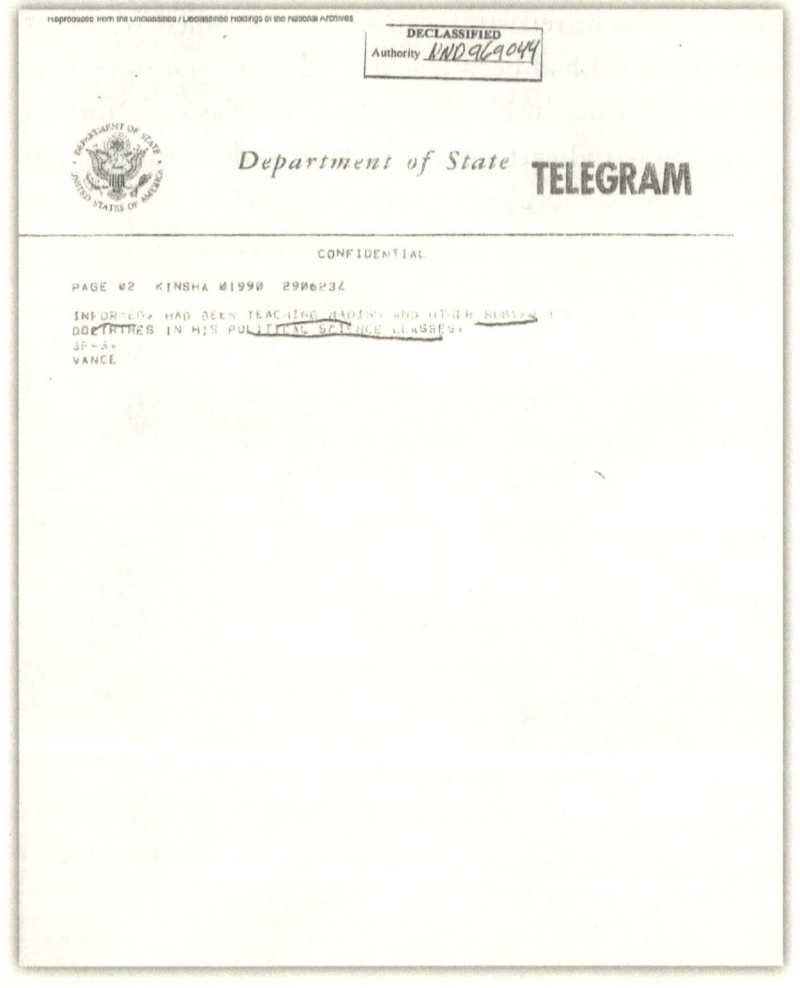

Ambassador Sheldon Vance's cable reporting on his meeting of March 26, 1971, with President Mobutu on "Trouble at University of Kisangani."

In the language of international politics, the president, whose government was a longtime U.S. "client," had brought my supposed offenses and his plans to deal with the USAID-subsidized university to the attention of his "patron." Informed by a dictator whom Henry Kissinger would later characterize as "ruthless"[11] that an American citizen had been teaching "Maoism and other subversive doctrines," the ambassador did not bring up the need for a fair process of judgment or suggest any kind of protection for me. And when I met with him three days later, he lied by telling me that my firing had come as "a complete surprise" to him.

In contrast to Ambassador Vance's initial reaction, the minister-counselor of the Belgian Embassy, Alfred Cahen, had taken a more forward stance even though he considered himself a longtime personal friend of Mobutu. Unlike the American Embassy staff, he had tried to meet me at the airport. After speaking with me on the telephone, he had driven to the house of the head of the Centre National de Documentation (CND), the Congolese intelligence office. As the chief was out, he had a beer with his wife and left behind a message. The following day, Alfred called to let me know that the CND man had told him that there was "just some university stuff" in my file, that in his judgment was "nothing serious."

A deeper understanding of the American Embassy's jaundiced attitude toward me, and one that is relevant to contemporary U.S. diplomacy, can be found in a 1987 Johns Hopkins University Ph.D. thesis by Elise Forbes Pachter: "Our Man in Kinshasa: U.S. Relations with Mobutu in 1970–83." After interviewing former members of the embassy and its Kisangani Consulate, Pachter determined that the officials considered me a troublemaker who "had been inciting students against the university administration" and had placed American diplomats "in the awkward position of having to protect a national being expelled by a "friendly regime."[12]

A week after my meeting with Minister Bulundwe, I was summoned to the office of the very man who had fired me and led the subsequent investigation: Vice-Minister of the Interior Claude Mafema. More relaxed than I had seen him earlier, he confided that he didn't like some of the people he had met at the university. Many of the Whites, he said, had been rude to him; he thought they were racists. Amid this unexpected camaraderie, he assured me that there were no charges against me. I could come and go as I pleased—even to Kisangani—but could not return to my job. I was to see the vice-minister of education, who would decide whether to transfer me to another university for the three months remaining in my contract or arrange for our return home. Shortly, the embassy cabled Washington: "Allegations made in press dropped due to Weissman explanations."[13]

Probably, I think now, the government never considered jailing or prosecuting me and a smooth ending was pre-ordained. Mobutu had shown his sensitivity to his patron's potential interest in my case by bringing it up with the ambassador. Moreover, the events at the university in distant Kisangani did not directly challenge his regime, although that might change should news of them infect the larger universities in politically sensitive Kinshasa and Lubumbashi. Perhaps Ambassador Vance's apparent complacency stemmed from his belief that the Mobutu regime would not take further action against me. If so, I wish he would have offered me and my family such reassurance.

On the other hand, Mobutu had demonstrated two years earlier at Lovanium that he would act forcefully if he judged that student militancy posed a potential political challenge.

And two months after my departure from the Congo, the army arrested a Belgian priest for leading a Lovanium University memorial service for the 1969 victims who had challenged the regime in its heartland.[14] In my case, the regime had been sufficiently concerned about the events in Kisangani, Congo's third largest city, to arrest half a dozen alleged student "ringleaders" who had been immediately flown to Kinshasa. So it is at least possible that by mobilizing the influential American and Belgian embassies to get involved in my case and furnishing the interior minister with an alternative explanation of my actions, I helped fend off more punitive treatment. I'll never know.

When I went to the Education Ministry there was no discussion of a temporary transfer to another university. I would be provided with our contractual air tickets back to the U.S. upon condition that I sign a statement that I was leaving voluntarily and not being expelled. The embassy subsequently cabled Washington: "As far as GDRC [Government of the Democratic Republic of the Congo] is concerned, case is closed."[15]

But it wasn't, either for President Mobutu or the U.S. government, as I would discover eight years later when I joined the staff of a congressional committee overseeing U.S. policy toward Africa.

~~~

PART II

Inside the Sausage Factory:
Washington, D.C.

CHAPTER 7

THE ROAD TO CONGRESS

W*e returned to the U.S.* in June 1971, following a two-month-plus detox in Spain, France, and England. We would have come back sooner, but my father-in-law, a tax lawyer, advised that if we did so we would be liable for taxes on the portions of our salaries that had been paid into our U.S. bank accounts. Unfortunately, I got home just in time to experience a collapsing political science job market, especially in my preferred areas of American foreign policy, international relations, and African politics. It did not help that I had been unable to be interviewed by interested universities while in Kisangani.

Luckily, within two months I was hired as an assistant professor by Jersey City State College (now New Jersey City University), across the Hudson River from New York City. Noticing my graduate studies in American government, the aging department chairman was anxious for me to inherit his innovative "Field Program in Practical Politics," which placed students in local political party organizations during election campaigns.

In addition to being desperate for a job, I was intrigued by the political situation in Jersey City, the second largest city in

New Jersey. One of the nation's classic, scandal-ridden urban political machines had been severely damaged by the mayor's conviction for extortion and conspiracy. It was being overtaken by a reform movement led by a thirty-year-old doctor who ran a drug rehabilitation center. This seemed like an interesting place to resume my political science career.

Over the next eight years, in teaching and research positions at Jersey City State, Stanford University, and the University of Texas in Dallas (UTD), as well as related consulting for governments and community organizations, I developed new specializations in U.S. urban politics and social programs. Most of my academic work and teaching focused on domestic U.S. government, responding to student interest and the bleak job prospects for foreign policy specialists.

At the same time, I continued to teach and write about American foreign policy toward Africa and the "Third World" of less-developed countries. In 1974 Cornell University Press published my book on U.S. Congo policy, *American Foreign Policy in the Congo 1960–1964*, which was well received by academic reviewers. In 1975, I was consulted by the staff of the U.S. Senate Select Committee on Intelligence, popularly known as the Church Committee, which was exploring past CIA covert action in the Congo. The following year, the Senate Foreign Relations Committee invited me to testify at a public hearing on a recently exposed CIA paramilitary campaign in neighboring Angola. The Congo, renamed "Zaire" as part of President Mobutu's African "authenticity" campaign, played a major role in that operation.

In 1977, I was asked to testify before the Africa Subcommittee of the House International Relations Committee concerning proposed U.S. "security assistance" to Zaire. This required me to think, for the first time, about a desirable *future* American policy toward that country. In 1978, the State Department invited me to make one of two major presentations to its "Zaire Discussion Group," which consisted of officials from various federal agencies, congressional staffers, academic experts, and businessmen. State also arranged for me to address a conference of American ambassadors to Africa on Belgian policy toward Zaire.

By then I was looking for a new job. In addition to interviewing for available academic positions—all on the domestic politics side—I journeyed from Dallas to Washington to inquire about possible Africa policy positions with the administration and Congress.

In undoubtedly the luckiest moment of my entire professional life, I walked into Brooklyn Congressman's Stephen Solarz's (D-NY) office the same day he learned that he would become Chairman of the House of Representatives Africa Subcommittee. Representative Charles Diggs (D-MI), who had headed the subcommittee for twelve years, had been convicted in federal court of diverting $70,000 of his congressional staff's salaries to his personal use. Although he had just won reelection, he agreed to step down from the chairmanship while his appeal was considered.

I knew Solarz from having testified before the subcommittee two years earlier. He had subsequently solicited my advice about whom to see during a planned trip to Southern Africa.

Steve proceeded to interview me for five hours, first in his office, then over dinner at his comfortable suburban estate. In his inimitable style, he politely but relentlessly interrogated me about all kinds of Africa policy issues, including a few I had never thought about. I was impressed, as this excerpt from the somewhat too flattering letter I wrote him afterward shows:

> Beyond our agreement on some basic substantive premises—African self-determination, the undesirability of both long-term Soviet client states and heavy-handed U.S. interventionism—I have great respect for your intellectual approach to policy problems: reflective, balancing the interests and consequences on either side, tuning in to the political realities yet taking advantage of the limited room for maneuver. . . . Even where . . . I stressed different nuances of a particular issue, I was struck by your open-mindedness and the strength of your arguments.

About a week after I returned to Texas, Steve called to offer me a job on the subcommittee staff. I would work with Johnnie Carson, a rare African American Foreign Service Officer he had met during a 1976 trip to Mozambique in Southern Africa. Johnnie would take a leave of absence from the State Department to become staff director. Steve enthused that the three of us were around the same age and would have fun working together to improve Africa policy.

Although I was in the midst of academic job interviews and had one good prospect, I quickly accepted Steve's offer, which seemed almost too good to be true.

I arrived in Washington in February 1979, on the eve of a historic snowstorm that paralyzed the city for days. Nancy, who had earned her master's degree in social work at Columbia

University and was employed at a community agency in Dallas, and Daniel would join me in June.

Our subcommittee Democratic majority staff office was located on the seventh floor of a rectangular white building two blocks south of the Capitol. Officially and boringly designated as "House Annex 1," it was popularly known as "the old Congressional hotel." In fact, one or two congressmen still lived there. Johnnie, David Frank (he would handle communications), staff assistant Sarah Lisenby (the lone Diggs holdover), and I were crammed into a large single room. There was little space between our simple brown wooden desks which were crowned with tall bookshelves. About five feet from the entrance there was a small black faux leather couch to receive visitors.

Our phones rang almost constantly. Spoiled by years of quiet professors' offices, I found the interruptions jarring. Another academic relic was my misplaced expectation that Sarah, our assistant, would answer my phone—which produced some tension between us. Decades afterward, she joked to our former colleagues that she had "trained me to answer the phone." As staff director, Johnnie had the modest privilege of dwelling in a closet with a door he could close for privacy. There was a separate minority staff office where our subcommittee's lone Republican staffer dwelt in similar circumstances.

I knew that my work would involve research, analysis, advocacy, and political strategizing. But despite my academic training in American government, I lacked a practical road map of *how* these functions should be carried out amidst a politically divided Congress, recalcitrant administration, and sometimes opinionated press. The subcommittee's metal file cabinets, which might have provided some guidance, were, I was disappointed to discover, empty. Further, the House's professional foreign affairs staffers received no orientation or training. Working closely with Steve, who was intellectually curious, well-informed, and energetic, albeit a novice subcommittee chairman, we sort of invented our jobs from scratch.

Although I shared the somewhat cynical perspective on American government characteristic of many political scientists, I was thrilled to find myself near the center of the action. Whether I was running across the street to Steve's office or down the block to the Foreign Affairs Committee's hearing rooms, striding over the gleaming tiled floor of the Capitol, alive with colorful geometric, floral, and classical designs, lolling on the grass-covered National Mall on a bright spring day, or attending a free Sunday afternoon concert at the Library of Congress, everything around me in those first few months seemed to herald the promise of my new position.

Looking back now upon the twelve years I would spend with the subcommittee staff, I believe that a good part of that promise was met. I got to play an important role in the enactment of some consequential legislation. This included maintaining economic sanctions against White-ruled Rhodesia while Great Britain was successfully leading negotiations for a democratic constitution that ended a long civil war; passing, over President Ronald Reagan's veto, economic sanctions against the White-led apartheid regime in South Africa, helping to pave the way for a peaceful transition to Black majority rule; facilitating an—alas—temporary negotiated settlement of the civil war in Angola along with a permanent end to U.S.

and Cuban military intervention there; and tripling food aid to Ethiopia and other desperate African countries as mostly American pop music stars sang out, "We Are the World."

These were exceptional initiatives for a Congress which, to this day, largely defers to the president on foreign policy. I was also involved with several other difficult policy issues, such as the conflict between Morocco and Algeria over self-determination of the Western Sahara; preventing genocide in Burundi; questioning military aid to authoritarian governments in Liberia, Kenya, Sudan, and Somalia; and reforming U.S. development assistance to Africa. Of these, we won some, lost some, and fell in between on others.

From my inside perch, I was able to observe various forces, often hidden from the public, that can hamper members of Congress with legitimate foreign policy concerns. (As a political scientist who had specialized in American government, I was getting a needed education on how Congress really worked.) No issue was more revealing of these constraints than U.S. policy toward Zaire. As our subcommittee's leading staffer on the country—subject to review by the staff director (until 1986 when I assumed that role), the chair, and various members—it was my business to not only be aware of these forces but also to suggest ways of overcoming them.

In this second engagement with the former Congo, I was on firmer ground than in Kisangani. I was in my own country and not embroiled in an explosive post-colonial racial conflict with uncertain consequences. To the contrary, our staff was well-integrated racially and collaborative. I served under two African American staff directors before succeeding to the post. And as a scholar of American government, I was well acquainted with relevant political norms and practices. No longer a man alone, I had the backing of a major congressional committee and the counsel and support of my staff colleagues.

Nevertheless, I again faced some tough choices. How should we in the subcommittee majority deal with distrustful members of the opposition party who held different perspectives on Zaire? What was the best strategy for coping with opposition from foreign and domestic lobbies, some of which were closely connected to members of our full Foreign Affairs Committee? How could we respond effectively to the State Department's often dubious defenses of its Zairian client regime? How should I personally react when my integrity, even loyalty, was questioned by high U.S. and Congolese officials and widely read conservative pundits? And what was I to do when President Mobutu, the head of the CIA, and certain State Department officials unexpectedly revived my "closed" case from Kisangani, casting doubt on my "objectivity"?

All of this meant that I would experience a second "coming of age" regarding Congo/Zaire, this time in my late thirties and forties. If the first iteration, in unfamiliar territory, had revealed me as a more emotionally-driven person than I'd previously realized and furnished me with a lifetime education in risk-taking, the second, on home grounds, would mold me into a more mature political actor.

～

CHAPTER 8

OUTSIDE EXPERTISE
IS NOT ENOUGH

During my time with Congress, Zaire posed a classic foreign policy dilemma, one we have seen in different forms in many countries important to American political and economic interests: for example, Cuba, the Philippines, Saudi Arabia, Honduras, El Salvador, Nicaragua, Ethiopia, and Egypt. Should the U.S. provide military or unrestricted economic aid to a historically close friend that is undermining its own political legitimacy and the goals of American assistance through massive corruption and gross violations of human rights? Doesn't such assistance also run the risk of amplifying U.S. identification with an unpopular, latently unstable regime, potentially complicating our relationship with its people and an eventual successor government?

Regarding Zaire, Washington officials' commitment to the government was undoubtedly strengthened by their awareness that the United States Central Intelligence Agency had twice, in 1960 and 1965, helped install Mobutu in power. The Zairian dictator wasn't just a longtime friend. He was "our man" in Kinshasa.

I got a sense of how much this special attachment influenced policymakers during my first month with the subcommittee. A top State Department official visited Steve in his office to appeal for increased military aid. After a while, not receiving the positive response he desired, he stood up to leave. Dramatically lowering his voice, he stated, "I don't know if I should tell you this, Congressman, but just between you and me, at a critical moment in the Congo crisis of the 1960s, Mobutu was willing to give us the help we needed."

I remember thinking, "Here was official, though private, confirmation of my research concerning the CIA's secret role in Colonel Mobutu's rise to power."

At our subcommittee's first public hearing on Zaire in March 1979, Assistant Secretary of State for African Affairs Richard Moose, representing the Democratic administration of President Jimmy Carter, attempted to resolve the policy dilemma by highlighting Western-sponsored economic, political, and military reforms being undertaken by the Mobutu government.

However, three scholars of Zaire's political economy were, in varying degrees, skeptical that the regime would adequately follow through with those reforms. The country was mired, these witnesses emphasized, from the presidency on down, in "institutionalized corruption," administrative incompetence, and personal rule, which produced mass misery. The army, including numerous unpaid soldiers, preyed upon the civilian population and misused foreign-supplied military equipment. As a result, there was a significant risk of violent political change. Among other things, the experts called for the U.S. to curtail its military assistance, not only to avoid condoning the army's abuses but, more importantly, to distance the U.S.

from a widely detested regime with which it was associated in the eyes of average Zairians. Even a symbolic cut in the modest military aid program, they indicated, might make it easier for the U.S. to establish good relations with a potential successor.

Consequently, the subcommittee, including six Democrats and three moderate Republicans, unanimously endorsed Steve's recommendation to reduce the administration's military aid request from $10.5 million to $0. On the other hand, we supported economic development and humanitarian aid targeted to benefit the people. These positions were consistent with a memorandum I had discussed with Steve and Johnnie exploring various policy options. Our subcommittee report made the further point that the elimination of U.S. military aid was unlikely to damage Zaire's self-defense. The military used American-financed jeeps and trucks for their private businesses and to extort the population. As for U.S.-funded spare parts for C-130 military transport planes, we had learned from the Defense Department that three of Zaire's six C-130s were inoperable due to deferred major maintenance and a fourth had been internally configured with a non-removable "VIP kit" for the president's personal, non-military use. In any event, France and Belgium were likely to continue to provide Zaire with training and other military assistance no matter what the U.S. did.[16]

Our recommendations cleared the full committee and went unchallenged on the House floor. But I soon discovered that our action, and my involvement in it, had provoked a response from President Mobutu. Toward the end of April, I received a letter from Alfred Cahen, now chief of staff to the Belgian foreign minister, congratulating me on my new job:

"You will be exactly the right man in the right place." He continued, tongue in cheek,

> As a matter of fact, you have been on the front pages since you took your job and I can remember that your good friend President Mobutu talked about you in the press conference he gave when he was last in Paris.

I scrounged up a news report of the Paris conference. As I recall, the president referred negatively to the subcommittee's position and briefly mentioned my allegedly troublesome conduct in Kisangani. I didn't assign much importance to his remark highlighting my role in the aid cut. Mobutu was aware of his government's bad image in the U.S. And he knew that Steve had traveled to Zaire a month before I was hired and publicly blasted corruption in the U.S. food aid program. I was actually a little encouraged by the president's comment on our subcommittee's action. By publicly elevating U.S. congressional criticism of his regime in the French press—which many well-educated Zairians followed—the president was furthering the very political distancing from his regime we were trying to achieve.

Our immediate problem was the upcoming committee conference to reconcile the differences between the House and Senate foreign aid bills. Steve's counterpart on the Senate Foreign Relations Committee, George McGovern (D-SD) had accepted the administration's military aid figure. As a former anti-war activist, I found that a bit shocking. McGovern, the Democrats' too-liberal presidential nominee against Republican Richard Nixon in 1968, had been a leader in the movement to end U.S. military intervention in Vietnam and Southeast Asia. But the senator seemed to buy the administration's arguments that Mobutu was undertaking reforms and accommodating him on military aid would help keep him on track. McGovern subsequently told me he had discussed the issue with one of Mobutu's lobbyists, William Blair, but insisted that did not influence his position. He did insert some hortatory language in the Senate aid bill about the need for progress toward a disciplined military force and that assistance should not be used for repression or contribute to corruption. However, the chairman of the Senate Committee, fellow anti-war liberal Frank Church (D-ID), took a rather dim view of McGovern's amendment: "We could add the Lord's Prayer to it for help," he opined. "We will need Divine intervention to see these objectives obtained. . . . Maybe," he ruminated, "we should consider doing what the House did."[17]

Church's words gave us some hope of prevailing in conference. Since the Senate Committee had not taken any testimony from non-governmental witnesses on Zaire, I encouraged one of ours to organize a letter to Committee members from U.S. experts. The resulting memorandum was signed by sixteen scholars, the principal American specialists on Zaire. It recommended that "no further American military assistance be extended to Zaire" because that would be "counterproductive to the United States national interest."

When I walked into the small room in the Capitol where the Conference Committee meeting was taking place, I felt kind of intimidated by the grandeur of the Senate conferees. Most of them—Church, Jesse Helms (R-NC), Jacob Javits (R-NY), John Glenn (D-OH)—were nationally prominent figures. In person, they looked larger than life. By comparison, the House representatives, even Committee Chairman Clement Zablocki (D-WI), were relative unknowns. I wondered if this imbalance was also felt by our members and would give the other side an advantage.

Our foreign aid conferences were prime examples of secretive governance. Whether or not the conferees voted formally to close these meetings to the public, they were effectively private because of the limited space provided. Although transcripts were eventually made available to the press and other outsiders, there was no real-time accountability.

As I waited for the Zaire issue to come up, I noticed an aide drop a note at Church's temporarily vacant spot at the conference table. As I was just a few feet away, I unabashedly got up, leaned over, and read it. It said that Morrison-Knudsen, a firm in the senator's home state of Idaho that had over 200 employees building a power transmission line in Zaire, had phoned "again" about preserving U.S. military aid. Returning to his seat, Church turned to an administration official to make a last-minute pitch for the $10.5 million (outside experts had no such privilege in these decisive conferences).

Deputy Assistant Secretary of State Lannon Walker offered a paean to a couple of limited Belgian and French military training programs. Steve did a good job, I thought, of challenging their effectiveness, using information I had obtained from the Defense Department, Belgian Embassy, and the press. Regarding the Zairian military, he warned, "History teaches us that this is an armed force that is feared by its own people. I think it is in our interest not to be formally identified with it."

Church, who had led the Senate's investigations of the CIA, including its assassination plots against Patrice Lumumba and covert paramilitary action programs in the Congo, responded, "Well, I equate very easily with that argument because it is so familiar to the liberal concept of the world and what our role should be in it."

But he went on to assert that "corruption is an endemic problem in Africa" and "we have seen governments far more reprehensible than Zaire." He doubted that our disassociation with the Mobutu regime would contribute to an end to the corruption. He seemed unaware of both the exceptional scale of government-led corruption in Zaire and the House's political distancing rationale.

Then the Senator got down to what seemed to be the heart of the matter for him:

> The question is: To what degree does a continuing contribution on our part tend to strengthen the forces upon which American citizens are relying? I remember the case of Morrison-Knudsen. They had to go in with their own air operation last time to get people out [during a rebel invasion of Shaba—formerly Katanga—Province in 1978]. If they had not been exceedingly adept, we would have lost more citizens there. *The company is pleading to have a continued show of American interest.* [Emphasis added]

It seemed that, in his effort to propitiate his home state company, Church was disregarding his previous critical comments on McGovern's encouragement of military reform,

Steve's arguments, and the advice of the Zaire specialists who had written to him.

In the end, the conference compromised at $8 million in military aid, a $2.5 million reduction from the administration's request. It provided that the funds would be allocated only if the president received "assurances" that they would not be used corruptly or to violate human rights, and so reported to Congress. However, Senator Javits, who composed this language on the spot, did not specify from whom such assurances would come.[18]

I thought we might have done better if Steve had not been so quick to float various financial compromises during the debate. He'd even offered to go up to $5 million before the conferees met. One of Steve's defining characteristics as a legislator was to take a very strong position while remaining prepared to resolve any major conflict by quickly moving toward an arguably premature compromise. (Once, during a conference on South Africa sanctions legislation, he sidled over to the chairman, Senator Richard Lugar (R-IN) and offered him a compromise that neither his House colleagues nor his Senate allies had discussed. Fortunately, amidst the din in the room, Lugar did not hear him.) But my main takeaway from the conference was that all the expertise we had mobilized in and out of the subcommittee through hearings and the academic specialists' letter proved less weighty than the interest of a single contractor in an important senator's state.

I met President Mobutu for the first time during his visit to Capitol Hill in September 1979. When foreign leaders came calling upon their American counterparts, the congressional foreign affairs committees were often asked to host them for private "teas." In our committee, these hour-long or so sit-down receptions, with waiters serving tasty desserts and beverages, usually drew more members than subcommittee hearings. They gave visiting dignitaries a platform to personally greet congressional decision-makers, present brief "talking points" on behalf of their policies, and answer a few questions. The questions were rarely challenging given the gracious setting. Having attended many of these teas with African leaders over the years, I cannot recall one where the guest of honor performed badly.

After the tea, Mobutu had arranged to meet Steve privately. The latter asked me to draw up a memo listing several congressional "expectations" which, if met, could lead to future increases in U.S. assistance. These included: improving pay and discipline within the military, reconciling with dissident Shaba Province, ending the "hemorrhaging" of foreign exchange from the export of coffee and diamonds and directing these recovered revenues toward the economic benefit and health of the Zairian people, and curtailing public officials' corruption.

As I prepared for the meeting, I got a frantic call from Steve's scheduler. He was delayed in returning to his office and she had just been informed that Mobutu was "lost" in their building. I hurried over to the Longworth Office Building to find a puzzled-looking Mobutu in the middle of a long corridor quite a way from Steve's office. A large, six foot or so tall figure in dark framed glasses, he stood out in his leopard skin cap, gray, *abacost* suit, cravat, and elaborately carved walking stick. I had no idea what to say to him! So, I focused upon my assigned role of guiding him through the turning corridors of this vast, rectangular building to Steve's office. When he was seated on the couch, I inquired whether he would like something to drink (a refrigerator in an adjoining room held sodas). He asked what I had to offer. The only sodas I could think of were the two soft drinks I had consumed in Kisangani—Coca Cola and Fanta Orange. He selected Fanta, which I carefully poured. Thankfully, Steve finally arrived and, soon afterward, an interpreter.

As I recall, the discussion was unremarkable except for one small thing. While responding to a point Steve raised, Mobutu turned toward me and said, "Your advisor knows about this and can inform you." To me, his comment indicated he knew something more about my background than old reports of my alleged provocations in Kisangani. His comment might even have contained a slight bit of respect. Needless to say, I was glad he did not bring up my past history.

When our subcommittee's Africa aid hearings resumed in early 1980, controversy broke out over the administration's new military assistance request for Zaire. Steve, Johnnie, and I had agreed that while conditions in the country had not improved, in view of the resistance we had encountered in conference, we would look more reasonable if we cut the administration's proposed $8 million to $4 million rather than again going down to zero.

During our Zaire hearing, the administration's cautious optimism about reform was supported by a historian of Africa chosen by the Republican minority. But it was strongly counterbalanced by testimony from the recently retired political counselor of the American Embassy in Kinshasa and a prominent political scientist specializing on Zaire.

In both the subcommittee and full committee, Congressman Floyd Fithian (D-IN) advocated in favor of the administration's request. His argument echoed the administration's contention that American military aid, in cooperation with the French and Belgian programs, was helping "leverage" a variety of economic and political reforms. In an intriguing addition, Fithian emphasized that it was in "our own security interest to have conditions prevail in Zaire as good as possible because of the cobalt source they represent for us and for the medical implants industry and lots of things." Fithian's staff aide enlightened me that his boss's interest in Zaire policy had been stoked by a hospital in his Indiana district that was concerned about future supplies of cobalt for medical treatment.

Imports from Zaire accounted for more than half of U.S. cobalt consumption. Fithian himself later told me that the hospital was "probably" being pushed by its cobalt supplier. Gosh, yet another American business lobby on the prowl. In our opinion, any Zaire government would, in its own economic interest, continue to provide its overwhelmingly Western markets with cobalt (at that time mainly used in jet engines) and other minerals. Should there be a temporary disruption of supply, the U.S. would cope through recycling, substitution, and tapping its strategic minerals stockpile.

When Fithian's amendment ran into resistance, Rep. Millicent Fenwick (R-NJ) suggested a compromise: chopping only $1.5 million instead of $4 million off the administration request. She said she detected a positive trend in actions bearing on human rights.[19]

Fenwick, a classic liberal Republican, was my favorite minority member during my time with the subcommittee.

An elegant woman of seventy who smoked a pipe during our hearings, she combined an aristocratic demeanor with a sincere concern for the welfare of average Africans. Many people thought she inspired the popular "Lacey Davenport" character in the comic "Doonesbury." (Cartoonist Gary Trudeau denied it.) Steve adored her. At our hearings the two frequently engaged in a kind of semi-flirtatious public repartee.

When I asked her staff aide about her new position on military aid—she had previously voted for $0—I was advised that it might well stem from her friendship with prominent lawyer David Morse, a lobbyist for the Zaire government. As a matter of fact, she once passed me an unsigned three-page document charting recent government reforms that looked, from its errors in English, like it could have been drafted by someone in the Zaire Embassy.

Whatever her true motivation, I worried that I might have contributed to her defection by preparing some inartful, emotionally-tinged questions for the administration at our hearing. I had been feeling increasingly frustrated by the administration's rationalizations for bolstering the Mobutu regime. So I relieved myself by preparing a series of queries that looked more like prosecutorial sorties. They were composed in the style of "You say in your statement. . . . But . . ." After the hearing, Fenwick asked me if I had drafted the questions. When I replied truthfully, she snapped, "I thought so." When I asked Steve what we could do to ease her concern over my objectivity, he replied (rather too facilely I thought), "Don't give the questions to the Republicans."

I didn't give up on Congresswoman Fenwick. At one point, I sent her a batch of credible reports on the political situation in Zaire. But her handwritten response suggested that I wasn't getting very far: "I was touched, but not surprised, that you should have sent me those 56 pages on the horrors of Zaire—and I count on you for a similar report on Mozambique."

Both Fenwick and our ranking Republican, Bill Goodling (R-PA), were uncomfortable that our subcommittee was targeting Zaire while approving administration requests for aid to other single-party, but less U.S.-friendly, regimes in Africa. In our defense, we supported only economic assistance to the latter, not military aid. Still, it was beginning to become clear to me that I needed to find ways of showing the Republicans that I respected where they were coming from if I were to have any hope of establishing some common ground.

In the end, our military aid reduction barely passed the full committee, which deadlocked 9 to 9 on the Fithian-Fenwick amendment. Here's how close we came to losing. Shortly before the vote, I asked Bruce Cameron, an Americans for Democratic Action human rights lobbyist I had met around the committee, to talk up our position with a moderate Republican, Rep. Joel Pritchard (R-WA), whom our staff and members had not been able to reach. Bruce went right up onto the committee dais—an area reserved for members and staff—and had a few words with him. Pritchard's "nay" vote on the amendment—the only one among committee Republicans—proved decisive. If outside expertise didn't work, I was learning, maybe well-connected insiders could make up for it. The tenuousness of our position was further exposed by the fact that four Democrats had joined with five Republicans in voting against us.

The ensuing House-Senate Conference partly resembled that of the previous year. Senators confessed their ignorance of the situation on the ground and depended upon an administration representative in the room to defend its military aid request of $8 million. Steve justified the House's 50 percent cut. What was different was that a new conferee, Senator Claiborne Pell (D-RI), leaned toward our position and the administration itself had allocated only $6 million—less than the previously authorized $8 million—to Zaire in the current fiscal year due to other worldwide needs. These developments made it relatively easy for the conferees to agree on a mid-point compromise of $6 million.

~~~

CHAPTER 9

A FEW PERSONAL
CHALLENGES

~~~

As I was trying to figure out how to cope with congressional opposition to our Zaire recommendations—and the narrow-based lobbies that helped fuel it—I was forced to deal with a variety of related personal attacks. Particularly during my first few years with the subcommittee, several important people raised questions about my objectivity and integrity, even whether I deserved my security clearance and would fulfill my oath to protect classified information. With strong support from my chairmen, I managed to survive those threats to my job and effectiveness. My odyssey is worth recounting because it sheds light upon some little known, highly questionable tactics that major government agencies, lobbyists, and media pundits employ to advance their foreign policy objectives. It also shows how I could and should have done more to lessen my vulnerability to such attacks.

1. Assistant Secretary Dick Moose Doesn't Like Me Anymore

As indicated earlier, before joining the subcommittee in 1979, I seemed in good odor with the State Department's

Africa Bureau, which was consulting me on Zaire policy. By the following year that seemed to have changed. In January 1980, my colleague Sarah accompanied a congressional delegation to Africa that was assessing possible threats to America's supply of critical minerals, including cobalt from Zaire's disaffected Shaba Province. I took the opportunity to entrust her with some questions for the U.S. consul in the provincial capital of Lubumbashi concerning the conduct of Belgian-trained government troops and the distribution of U.S. food aid there, as well as a reported massacre of diamond miners in neighboring Kasai Province. I later heard that Assistant Secretary Moose and others in the Africa Bureau had construed my initiative as a sneaky effort to elicit information through a "back channel" rather than going through the U.S. Embassy in Kinshasa. My assurance to the consul that his "answers would be on a background basis, non-attributable in any way" was taken as a "work-around" of the ambassador.

In March I wrote Moose explaining that I had provided Sarah with questions I would have myself asked the consul had I been present. I mentioned a trip Steve and I had taken to Morocco where we had posed numerous off-the-record questions to the U.S. consul in Casablanca to get his individual reading of the political situation and flesh out the written embassy reporting we had seen. I assured the assistant secretary that my questions were "not intended to suggest that [the consul] should say things contrary to embassy perspectives." And I pointed out that when the Congo Desk officer had informed me of the bureau's negative reaction, I had agreed with her that the "non-attribution" language "would have been best omitted." Regrettably, I received no response from Moose.

The following month, when I approached him after a hearing, he stunned me by issuing a blanket condemnation of my behavior and integrity. When I asked him to explain, he brought up that I had attacked him behind his back at an academic panel on Africa policy that I moderated at a meeting of the African Studies Association (ASA) a few months earlier. As I tried to respond, he cut me off and walked away. At the time, I was working with Johnnie and Moose and his staff on our subcommittee's campaign to preserve the Carter administration's economic sanctions against White minority-ruled Rhodesia. There was now a visible strain in some of our meetings. One day Johnnie smilingly mentioned that Moose had called me an "academic pinhead."

I quickly wrote him again, explaining what had actually happened at the ASA meeting. As a member of the association's Current Issues Committee, I had invited Moose to discuss U.S. policy toward Africa. After he unexpectedly departed following his presentation, leaving his deputy, Lannon Walker, behind to answer questions, the other members of his panel offered their views. Then, I continued,

> I briefly departed from my moderator role to correct what I felt was an incomplete picture [by him] of Congress's reputed lassitude in Africa policy. Upon concluding, I turned to Lannon and asked if he would like to comment. He declined. I was sorry to learn at the last minute that you would be leaving early and would have offered my personal comment directly if you had stayed longer. Certainly, its phrasing was in the spirit of moderate difference and not of personal attack.

Moose didn't answer that letter either.

I discussed the situation with Steve, who nonchalantly assured me, "You'll be around here a lot longer than him." It was true. After several months, Moose departed, along with the outgoing Democratic administration. But had he stayed on, with our split unresolved, my Africa work would have been more difficult.

What was I to take from these seemingly trivial misunderstandings? Did the fault lie with the egos or bureaucratic maneuverings of certain State Department officials? Did the subcommittee's dissident position on Zaire provoke undue suspicion of my actions? More likely, I had failed conform to some unwritten norms of appropriate congressional-executive branch relations such as going through the embassy hierarchy or deferring to the administration in off-the-Hill public presentations. In any event, I needed to be more careful to detect and avoid potential taboos.

2. The Head of the CIA Complains About Me

In June 1980 I stepped onto a commercial plane that would carry Steve, Johnnie, and me to South Africa on a legislative fact-finding mission. Steve immediately drew me aside, saying he had just had a discussion about me with Admiral Stansfield Turner, the CIA director. Turner had mentioned that his officers were "nervous" about meeting with me—which they had been doing for over a year in Washington, D.C. intelligence briefings as well as at American embassies during some of my trips abroad—notwithstanding my Top Secret security clearance for classified information. I must have looked quite stricken, for Steve quickly added, "Don't worry, you're not going to be fired."

Turner had expressed three concerns. I had published an article in a recent book edited by leftist critics of the agency that included an appendix claiming to disclose the identity of undercover CIA officers in Africa. I had recently telephoned undercover CIA personnel. And nine years ago, I had gotten into trouble at the university in Kisangani and been forced to leave the country.

In the rushed atmosphere of boarding the aircraft, I offered Steve some quick explanations, elaborating further in a letter after we returned from South Africa.

In the first place, my article in the book *Dirty Work 2: The CIA in Africa,* was a version of a scholarly article on CIA covert action in Congo and Angola that I had published twice before: in a 1977 academic volume and a 1979 political science journal. I had given the *Dirty Work* editors permission to reprint an editorially abridged version in what they described to me as "a collection of articles on Africa." I had no foreknowledge that the book would contain an appendix—based essentially on unclassified State Department and other biographical registers—purporting to identify CIA officers in Africa. After the volume appeared, I called Ellen Ray, one of the two editors who had approached me, to complain. She apologized for not having fully informed me of the details of the project.

Had I known about the appendix, I would certainly have reconsidered my permission in view of my new job. In granting it I was aware that the original academic publisher had consented to the reprint as had that book's editor, a prize-winning Africanist scholar and former consultant to the U.S. Defense Intelligence Agency. I also knew that the *New York Times* had granted permission to reprint an article by renowned journalist Seymour Hersh and that other respected journalists were represented.

Regarding Admiral Turner's second concern, I told Steve that I was unaware of having telephoned any undercover personnel—with one possible exception. Our subcommittee staff had been working on an investigation of U.S. agencies' performance in the notorious case of a Vermont company's breach of the U.S. arms embargo against South Africa. As the CIA was one of the agencies under review, I had called the Agency to try to reach Dorwin Wilson, who had been identified in the press as the retired, former chief of the CIA Station in South Africa. The paper that had broken the scandal, the *Burlington Free Press*, had referenced a conversation between Wilson and its reporter. I was told that Wilson was not there, and he did not return my call. I did not try again.

Lastly, I provided Steve with a brief, oral history of the events in Kisangani, including the final acceptance of my explanation by the Mobutu government. He smiled and gently commented, "I can understand why you didn't put that on your resume."

I was fortunate to have the right boss. Steve had worked closely with me for a year and a half and had confidence in me. He accepted my explanation without further investigation. A different subcommittee chairman, one who did not know me as well or was more anxious to please a powerful official, might have fired me or insisted that I produce documents and witnesses to back up my story.

Steve got back to Turner, who dropped the matter. However, his intervention got me thinking about whether anyone at the CIA might have contributed to a couple of negative press articles about me in 1979 and 1980. A month after I joined the subcommittee, Cord Meyer, a veteran high-level CIA officer who had recently retired and become an opinion columnist for the *Washington Star*, charged, inaccurately, that certain queries directed to the administration during our recent Zaire hearing "clearly implied that drastic cuts should be applied with the aim of hastening Mobutu's downfall." . . .

"Some of this questioning," he suggested, "may not have been entirely motivated by a disinterested search for objective truth."

Meyer singled me out as a former professor who had written "a monograph that reveals his bias. Having predicted Mobutu's inevitable overthrow he has a stake in the adoption of a policy that would prove him right."[20] He appeared to be referring to the paper I presented at the private State Department conference in 1978, in which I had cautioned (consistent with the opinions of other Zaire specialists): "There is a strong possibility that the weakened regime will disappear within the next few months or years. . . ." In chatting with me on the phone, Meyer had not asked about my "monograph" or whether the subcommittee was attempting to displace Mobutu, which it was not.

An even more flawed piece by the internationally known foreign affairs columnist Robert Moss appeared in the British *Daily Telegraph* in late 1980. Moss alleged that "Steven [sic] Weissman," a "key advisor" to Solarz on issues regarding Morocco, Zaire, and Angola, was a "foremost supporter" of ex-CIA officer Philip Agee, who had turned against the agency, exposing covert operations and personnel. Moss charged that I had written articles, including with Agee, that had blown the cover of agency officers.[21] After I contacted him, Moss, to his credit, publicly confessed his error. "There is egg over a number of faces, including mine, because of a case of mistaken identity in Washington," he subsequently wrote. He apologized, acknowledging I was "not the same Mr. Weissman who assisted the CIA's ideological defector." . . . "My sources" he explained, "*usually reliable intelligence analysts* [emphasis added], have been appropriately chastised."[22]

Notwithstanding Moss's *mea culpa*, for a couple of years afterward I heard from staff colleagues that some State Department officers believed I was the "other" Weissman who had allegedly aided Agee.

I found a sympathetic ear in Bob Kelso, the CIA's liaison with our committee. I asked Bob what I could do to allay residual suspicion in his agency. His recommendation was simple: "Just work your way through it." It proved to be sound advice. I received many Agency briefings in succeeding years from both intelligence analysts and covert operations officers; I had no sense that they were withholding information because of my alleged past conduct.

3. "Errors and No Facts" and the Fight for the Africa Subcommittee Chairmanship

In the 1980 elections the Republicans gained control of the presidency and Senate; the House remained Democratic. In early 1981, the chairmanship of the Asia Subcommittee opened up and Steve decided to take it. I had drafted a memo from our staff, self-interestedly advising him to stick with Africa where he was likely to have a greater impact under the Ronald Reagan administration. He did not take our advice, but even with his new position, he continued to exert influence on Zaire and other African issues in the committee and Congress.

At first it was unclear who his successor would be. By the tradition of seniority, the Africa post was destined for centrist Dan Mica (D-FL). However, some committee Democrats, including members of the Congressional Black Caucus such as subcommittee member William Gray (D-PA) preferred the more liberal Howard Wolpe (D MI), who had strongly supported Steve's thrust on the subcommittee. Their concern was heightened by the election of the conservative Reagan. We staffers, with our jobs probably on the line, got into the act. Returning home from a congressional trip to an African-American conference in Sierra Leone, we encouraged members of the delegation, which Gray headed, to support Howard or another liberal.

Howard was a milder-mannered, less driving personality than Steve. He had been active on numerous African issues, including Zaire. I was also comfortable with him because he had been an established Africanist scholar before entering politics. Having lived in Nigeria and published a book on politics there, and having taught African Politics at Western Michigan University, he had an instinctive grasp of the ethnic and social currents swirling beneath the continent's political institutions. I also liked the fact that he was more of a pure liberal in foreign policy than Steve, though the latter had a better knack for constructing narrow arguments that appealed to centrists.

One day before the crucial committee vote on the chairmanship, the *Washington Post* published a column by the syndicated columnists Rowland Evans and Robert Novak that appeared in 233 newspapers. It was titled, "Still Going After the CIA."[23] It announced its theme up front: "Trying to repeal the 1980 election and preserve Jimmy Carter's human rights policies, liberal Democratic congressmen are plotting to keep control of the House Foreign Affairs African subcommittee and retain as a symbol of the past a staffer named Steven [sic] R. Weissman." Claiming that "backroom fighting over Solarz's successor reached a frenzied peak over the weekend," with Speaker of the House Thomas "Tip" O'Neill weighing in for Mica over the less senior Wolpe, the columnists zeroed in on Wolpe's assurance to Solarz that he would keep the existing majority staff—particularly me. I was mentioned in nine of the article's thirteen paragraphs.

Wolpe's decision to retain me was portrayed as "a quixotic attempt to repeal the election and restore politics of the '60s and '70s. The role of Weissman, so distrusted by the government of Zaire that he is regarded as an enemy by that U.S. ally, shines as a *beau ideal* of the post-Vietnam mood. But that time has passed."

How far it had passed was, the columnists wrote, "demonstrated" by CIA Director Turner's "admonishment" of Solarz that my contribution to *Dirty Work 2* "had tended to tighten the tongues" of CIA briefers. Like Moss, Evans and Novak associated me with Philip Agee who, they noted, had written an introduction to that volume. While reporting my denial of foreknowledge of Agee's introduction and the controversial appendix, they cast doubt upon it by emphasizing that I had not informed Solarz of my contribution to the book until Turner brought it up. They mischaracterized my essay, which was a critique of the assumptions behind specific past CIA "covert action" programs in Zaire and Angola, as "an attack on [all] CIA undercover work in Zaire," which would include traditional information collecting. Were some of these charges the result of another possible CIA press leak, one akin to Meyer or Moss's columns?

Like Dick Moose, the columnists found something not to like in my performance at an obscure scholarly meeting. They maintained that during the most recent ASA conclave I had used my "subcommittee position to attack Zaire in a way surpassing the latitude taken by members of Congress themselves" by telling a "largely black audience . . . 'Zaire is a basket case. . . . It is falling apart . . . A concentrated lobbying effort is what is needed in Washington to change policy." This account was from "an eyewitness who took careful notes."

"Those and other Weissman comments," Evans and Novak continued, "look to the government of Zaire suspiciously like an attempt by a U.S. government official to destabilize their country."

I immediately called and wrote Meg Greenfield, the editor of the *Post* editorial page, requesting an opportunity to respond to "this reckless and unprofessional attack on my reputation." After I detailed my grievances and explained that the committee would vote the next day on the chairmanship, she agreed to publish my approximately five hundred-word letter to the editor that morning.[24] In it, I emphasized that Evans and Novak had disregarded relevant information I had provided to them by phone and messenger that:

> ⸱ My contribution to the book was an abridged reprint of a previously published article;

▹ I had complained to the editor when I learned about its appendix;

▹ I had asked Evans to call that editor to verify my story, but he refused to do so;

▹ The African Studies event was a small academic panel with a largely White, not Black, audience;

▹ Reed Kramer, the editor of the respected periodical *Africa News*, had informed me that a tape recording of the event showed that the report of my comments had been torn out of context and was partially inaccurate;

▹ Evans had rejected my request that he contact the three other members of the ASA panel because he "believed" his source's notes;

▹ I had said nothing at the meeting inconsistent with public subcommittee perspectives on Zaire.

Soon after the column appeared, I received a note from probably the most moderate academic critic of the Zaire regime, Professor Crawford Young of the University of Wisconsin. He called the Evans and Novak column a "scurrilous piece," adding that "most people that I know who attended the panel found your remarks careful and judicious. It would be intriguing to know who was taking notes at the proceedings at the ASA; it was evidently someone who was unable to tell black from white."

Considering the columnists' reference to how the Zaire government viewed my alleged remarks, I suspected their source concerning the ASA meeting might have been someone from the Zaire Embassy or one of Zaire's American lobbyists.

The PEN American Center wrote the *Post*: "Evans and Novak engage in a kind of baiting that attempts to ascribe un-Americanism to anyone concerned about human rights and its relation to American foreign policy. . . . Beyond that, it is scandalous to suggest that the exercise if free speech . . . is itself an attempt to destabilize a government."

I decided to call my letter to the editor to the attention of the syndicate that sponsored Evans and Novak's column. To my surprise, it agreed to distribute it to its outlets. I know that it appeared in the *Dallas Morning News* because a former colleague at the University of Texas at Dallas sent it to me. Still, I understood that my letter would receive far less attention than the original column, which reached millions.

Overcoming Evans and Novak's intervention, Howard narrowly captured the subcommittee chairmanship by a vote of 11–8 of the Committee's Democratic Caucus. Concerned about potential Republican reactions to Howard's decision to keep me, I asked Steve to send my letter to other committee members and enter it into the *Congressional Record*. He did so, writing in the *Record* that the columnists' "allegations are completely unfounded and, in fact, amount to little more than a pathetic parody of the vicious techniques associated with McCarthyism."

While I was relieved by this denouement, I knew I had dodged a bullet. Howard could justifiably have perceived me as an unnecessary burden in his quest for the chairmanship. I was not as close to him as to Steve. Unlike Steve, he represented a competitive congressional district. His continued employment of a staffer whom, it had been suggested, belonged to "the anti-CIA cult" might be weaponized by a future Republican opponent. But he backed me up, passing on letters from Africanist scholars urging him to keep me on.

A liberal Democratic staff colleague congratulated me on surviving "Errors and No Facts." Still, I soon had reason to believe that the column had damaged my reputation among some relevant audiences. Indeed, one Republican committee member inserted the column in the *Record,* though he later apologized to Howard, blaming his staff. More concerning, a year later a couple of remarks by our subcommittee's moderate ranking Republican, Bill Goodling, suggested that I was still paying a political price for the column.

I had been the principal author of a subcommittee majority staff study, "The Space Research Case and the Breakdown of the U.S. Arms Embargo against South Africa." Its conclusions were shocking and quite relevant to overall U.S. arms control policy. From 1976 to 1978, Space Research Corporation, a Vermont company, sold and shipped to South Africa 60,000 155mm extended range artillery shells, at least four 155mm guns, and technology that enabled South Africa to establish its own manufacturing and testing capability.

Notwithstanding the official U.S. policy since 1963 of embargoing arms to the apartheid regime, the State Department Office of Munitions Controls had misapplied its own export regulations to authorize the transfers of so-called "rough forgings." Moreover, the U.S. Army approved the manufacturing of the shells in its own facility without verifying their destination. The report further concluded that it was "probable" that a U.S. defense consultant assisting the CIA's covert action program in Angola—who bore the unlikely name of Jack Frost—had informed South African officials that they could obtain superior artillery from the U.S. company. We therefore recommended several measures to improve the enforcement of arms embargoes worldwide.[25]

I was proud of our staff work. My analysis had been based on documentation from six federal agencies, records of the federal investigation specially released to us by the U.S. District Court in Vermont, and interviews with fifty individuals from government agencies, Space Research Corporation, its banker, and other informed sources.

We scheduled a hearing to consider the report's bearing on current enforcement of the South African embargo. But Goodling, who had been a pretty cooperative ranking member of the subcommittee for three years, wrote Howard complaining that his minority staff aide, Gardner Peckham, had only recently been made aware of the investigation. In addition, he stated, "The report was authored by a single majority staff member, and I might add, clearly reflects the staff member's lack of objectivity."

Howard wrote back, refuting Goodling's claim that Gardner had not been consulted in a timely way. He pointed out that three members of the subcommittee staff and one full committee staffer had been involved in the three-year investigation. which had been monitored by Johnnie, who reviewed and edited the final report. Nonetheless, I was disturbed by the top subcommittee Republican's negative opinion of my work and made an appointment to see him.

I spent much of my first substantive conversation with Rep. Goodling in three years attempting to convince him that I sought to objectively collect and analyze the facts of the case. I got so wrapped up in my self-justification that I felt my eyes filling with tears. I told him the reason I had come to Washington was to apply my academic skills to real-world problems. I was trying desperately to get through to someone who had himself been an educator before coming to Congress. But rather than engaging with me on the substance of the report or other subcommittee issues, Goodling smiled and observed, "You know, you're famous among the committee's Republicans." I understood this as a probable reference to the lasting impact of the Evans and Novak piece on his colleagues.

Yet Goodling's complaint also provoked some needed soul-searching on my part. Sure, we majority staffers had done the minimum to keep Gardner informed about what we were doing and planning. But I could have been more forthcoming with him sooner about our conclusions. Considering the problems I had already experienced with Rep. Fenwick, it was obvious that I would have to do a better job of reaching out to the minority in the future.

4. State Department Officials Reinterpret My Kisangani Experience to Discredit the Subcommittee's Critique of U.S. Policy toward Zaire

My most enduring personal challenge was a rather widely circulated myth among State Department officers working on Zaire. It postulated that my criticism of U.S. policy toward the Mobutu regime was the product of a "grudge" I was carrying against the Zairian president after getting "PNG'd" (i.e., declared *persona non grata*) from Zaire. In her aforementioned dissertation drawing upon interviews with department officials, Pachter concluded: "Policy makers disliked Weissman because they felt he had enlisted Congressmen in his personal vendetta against Mobutu." One official told her:

> Weissman played particularly well to Solarz in helping him find an issue with which to divide himself from the Carter administration, and Steve's personal animosity toward Mobutu and the Mobutu regime fit well . . . The degree of vindictiveness in his discussion of Zaire and the all-consuming passion he has for Zaire seem to indicate that the incident created a crusade . . . his primary aim seems to be to embarrass Mobutu and preferably overthrow him.[26]

As late as 2001, a decade after I had left the subcommittee staff, I heard about a variation of this theme. Nancy was seated at a dinner next to Ken Brown, a retired Foreign Service Officer who had headed the State Department regional office for the Congo from 1980 to 1981 and subsequently served as deputy assistant secretary of state for Africa from 1987 to 1989. During their conversation, he remarked, "We all thought Steve was being hard on Zaire out of revenge against the U.S. government because he felt the embassy didn't support him enough when he got in trouble in Kisangani." Nancy rather authoritatively informed him, "You don't understand Steve; he doesn't hold grudges."

Both versions of my "vendetta" ignored some key facts. It was the ULC administration as much as the government that had forced my exit from Kisangani. And according to the U.S. Embassy's own cable, the Congolese minister of the interior "accepted" my explanation of the Mao excerpt and the government "closed" my case. Finally, I had mobilized a seemingly indifferent U.S. Embassy to "show the flag" in the minister's office to facilitate my safe departure, which occurred.

Equally problematic were the assumptions that my analysis of Zaire was based on revenge rather than on research and my overall liberal prospective on foreign policy, and that I had "poisoned the Congressional well"—as if Steve, Howard, and other House members would have taken different positions toward the corrupt, repressive Mobutu regime, but for my machinations.

Interestingly, Pachter attributed these officials' views of my role to a broader psychological mechanism of "cognitive dissonance" they developed in response to the negative environment they encountered in Zaire and Congress. They were, she maintained, "resolving discomfort by reformulating reality":

> Weissman's attacks on Mobutu became the subject rather than the Mobutu regime itself. Discrediting Weissman allowed policy makers to avoid the discomfort of defending someone they knew to be corrupt, and to turn their attention to the attacker rather than the subject of the attack.[27]

At least the State Department's largely internal rehashing of my sojourn in Kisangani was not as threatening to my job or effectiveness as spears thrown outward to Congress and the public by the CIA and Evans and Novak. Yet it was disturbing to see that many intelligent Foreign Service officers trafficked in unsubstantiated rumor. What might this suggest about the State Department's general proficiency in information-gathering?

Most of the State Department's Washington-based Congo desk officers I sought information from seemed to recognize their responsibility to be as honest as possible with Congress. Still, I sensed a certain hostility from some State Department officials, even ones I worked with on non Zaire issues. Ever the optimistic rationalist, I decided to draft a letter in June 1983 to members of State's Africa and Congressional Relations Bureaus deflating the Kisangani myth. Howard advised me not to send it, saying it would probably prolong rather than end the argument. Reluctantly, I buried it in my files.

As the years went by, the issue faded, although it never entirely disappeared. Thus, in February 1990 the conservative journalist David Brock—who subsequently renounced his career as a "Right Wing Hit Man"—penned an article in *The American Spectator* attacking congresspersons critical of President Mobutu. His piece contained some new twists on the State Department myth: "Weissman, the Committee staff director, was thrown out of Zaire by Mobutu's government for publicly criticizing the government when he was a Peace Corps volunteer in the 1960s, and he has harbored a grudge ever since."

Brock cited no sources for his disinformation. I was able to publish a letter to the editor laying out the author's errors and noting that Mobutu's minister of the interior was helpful to me at the end. Brock remained unmoved and unsourced: "I fail to see," he replied, "why saying Mr. Weissman was in

the Peace Corps rather than at a university should constitute defamation. Further, I don't see how this changes the
aptness of my observation that Mr. Weissman's unfortunate
personal experiences in Zaire continue to shape his zealous
views today."[28]

~~~

CHAPTER 10

THE REAGAN ADMINISTRATION REFUSES TO ACCEPT A CONGRESSIONAL DEFEAT

———

*A*s *Howard took over* the subcommittee chairmanship in the Democratic House in early 1981, the
new Republican administration assumed power. At our foreign
aid hearings, Acting Assistant Secretary of State for African
Affairs Lannon Walker announced new foreign policy principles that heralded increased military aid for Mobutu. The
Reagan administration wanted "national security interests"
to be "a major determinant" in foreign assistance decisions; it
particularly wished to demonstrate "that it pays to be America's
friend." It would take some time, though, for the new regime
to fully apply these standards to Zaire. It requested $10.5 mil-
lion in military aid, the same figure the Carter administration
had proposed two years earlier.

In formulating its recommendations, the subcommittee
argued that Western-supported reform efforts had clearly been
overwhelmed by the political environment. The Pentagon and
U.S. intelligence agencies confirmed press reports that even

the small numbers of French and Belgian-officered troops were deprived of adequate logistic support due to corruption. And modest hopes for increased accountability through the advisory, one-party legislature were evaporating.

The latter's most outspoken members, the "Group of 13" were arrested and banished to internal exile after calling for a national roundtable of political factions and non-violent, democratic change. In addition, the International Monetary Fund (IMF) effort to control foreign exchange leakages from official channels, reported by Zaire's own auditors to amount to hundreds of millions of dollars annually, was a widely acknowledged bust.

Prudently taking into account the previous year's legislative struggle, Howard and the subcommittee again recommended $4 million in military aid.[29] This time there was no opposition, either in committee or on the House floor. As usual, the Senate committee acquiesced to the administration's higher figure ($10.5 million).

My reeducation in American government continued when The House-Senate Conference on Foreign Aid convened in December. There, Howard focused on the Zaire military's misuse of American equipment to extort and abuse the population which, despite ongoing Belgian and French military training and equipment programs, believed that the American superpower was the prime supporter of the widely disliked regime.

A general representing the administration admitted, "It is true that we have had some difficulties with this program. We have to remember that we are not providing the primary military support for Zaire . . . the amounts of money . . .

proposed are barely adequate to support the equipment that is now in the country." Rep. Don Bonker (D-WA), chairman of the Human Rights Subcommittee, retorted, "If we are concerned about cost-effectiveness, I think any amount of money for military assistance is wasted . . . because the army now is the most corrupt and inefficient in all of Africa." Howard, backed by Chairman Zablocki, suggested a compromise of $6 million, the amount the conference had approved the previous year and the administration had allocated the year before that.

The new Republican Senate Foreign Relations Committee Chairman Charles Percy (R-IL) responded:

> I would at least like to make the point on the record . . . that from my standpoint I think I could live with the $6 million, but that is not a limitation on it, and they could go above it if they have to.

It was "good sense," he observed, to support a largely French-Belgian effort by funds which would be conducive to "better maintenance" of military equipment. Therefore, he continued, "I would frankly like to stand firm on the Senate figure of $10.5 million." He added that he had discussed the subject with President Mobutu during his visit to Capitol Hill a couple of weeks earlier. He was encouraged that the president was willing to invite "Amnesty International inspectors" into the country. Having stated his preference, Percy then concluded with this response to the proposed Zablocki-Wolpe compromise: "So I would accept the $6 million figure, but also with the feeling that progress is being made, although I am really quite supportive of what the administration is trying to do there in that area."

Trying to nail down the compromise and move on, Zablocki seized upon Percy's applause for "progress . . . being made," saying, "And I think we ought to have that in the report language" (i.e., the Conference Report). Percy assented, "If we would incorporate that in the report I would feel better about it." Zablocki then stated, "Without objection, that is agreed to. There is agreement on the figures of the military amounts." Percy stated, "There is no objection on our side."[30]

The Conference Report that passed both Houses of Congress read: "The conference substitute is a compromise whereby $6.0 million is recommended for Zaire." Senate committee staff had proposed adding, in the vein of Percy's initial remark, "this recommendation is not a ceiling." However, their proposal was rejected by House committee staff in view of Percy's final acceptance of Zablocki's compromise figure. Oddly, the report omitted the conferees' agreement to add language referring to "progress" by the Zaire government.

A couple of weeks later, I learned that, despite the language in the report, the administration was planning to allocate the full $10.5 million request to Zaire. Howard promptly wrote the new assistant secretary of state for African affairs, Chester Crocker, reiterating the conference's decision. He noted that, under committee precedents, the use of the word "recommendation" in the report only allowed the administration flexibility to increase aid under "extraordinary circumstances (e.g., a Cuban invasion or change in government in Zaire)."

Chairman Zablocki wrote similarly to Secretary of State Alexander Haig. Eight of the nine members of our subcommittee, including three Republicans, also wrote Crocker, warning that if the administration proceeded with the $10.5 million they would have to "earmark" future aid to Africa, eliminating any flexibility in extraordinary circumstances. Every subcommittee chair signed an even broader caution to Haig that if the administration went ahead, "We will have to strongly reconsider our current caution about earmarkings in future Foreign Assistance legislation."

At the same time, Percy, joined by the new Africa subcommittee chairperson, Senator Nancy Kassebaum (R-KS), wrote Crocker offering a different view of the conference decision. They quoted a portion of Percy's initial comment that $6 million was not a "limitation," but omitted that he prefaced it as an effort to "at least make a point on the record . . . from my standpoint." Most importantly, they ignored his final decision: "So I would accept the $6 million figure but also with the feeling that progress is being made," and his "no objection on our side" comment, after Zablocki moved that the conference approve the "military amounts" he and Howard had proposed.

Taking advantage of the Senators' letter, the administration invoked "a difference of opinion within Congress" to justify moving forward on its own.

This was not the only time I witnessed an alleged vagueness in a conference transcript being seized upon by an administration and its congressional allies to overcome Congress's will. It happened twice in connection with conferences on South African legislation. One time, it had the effect of tempering our subcommittee's effort to steer U.S. economic aid to South African education toward programs supported by anti-apartheid groups. On another occasion, it narrowed the scope of U.S. economic sanctions on steel imports from apartheid South Africa. Not that administrations and congressional partisans were the only parties at fault. In all three cases, the problem might have been averted if the conferees had a norm permitting a senior staffer to stand up for a minute and clarify the decision that had been reached.

Not content with the $10.5 million it had squeezed out, the administration next tried to coax an additional $5 million from the House and Senate Foreign Operations Appropriations Subcommittees via an obscure process called "reprogramming." However, the Democratic-controlled House subcommittee blocked the maneuver.

~~~

CHAPTER 11

PRESIDENT MOBUTU PLAYS
THE ISRAELI/JEWISH CARD

$\sim$

In September 1981, shortly before the conference, our subcommittee had taken dramatic public testimony from Nguza Karl-i-Bond, Mobutu's former prime minister. Nguza had resigned and fled to Belgium where he denounced the regime's corruption and human rights abuses. After reading in the Belgian press that he planned to come to the United States, I suggested to Howard that he invite Nguza to meet with our subcommittee. He did so, and Nguza agreed to testify at a public hearing.

In discussions with the latter's American intermediary, I emphasized the necessity of documenting any allegations he might level at the regime. Shortly before the hearing, I met with Nguza, the intermediary, and an allied former Zairian official to acquaint them with the format, the subcommittee's interests, and the administration's anticipated arguments. While I did not "coach" Nguza on the substance of his testimony, I certainly gave him more of the "lay of the land" than we normally furnished subcommittee witnesses. I was probably violating an unwritten committee norm but considered it low risk since it took place in a private setting. To my mind, the importance of the opportunity justified this minor trespass.

Nguza provided some of the best formulated and most credible testimony I heard on any African country in my years with the subcommittee. He described how, in his previous incarnation as foreign minister, he had been charged with "treason" during the rebel invasion of Shaba, his home province. Diplomatic pressure from the Carter administration, he said, had helped him emerge from prison (where he had been tortured), and resume his position. He specified the reforms Western governments had demanded of Mobutu and his failure to implement them.

In this connection, Nguza submitted documents from a secret parliamentary inquiry showing that Mobutu, his family, and close associates withdrew $150 million in foreign exchange from the Central Bank between 1977 and 1979. He further submitted that when he became prime minister, he was officially informed that the bank had transferred $30 million to Mobutu's personal account and that state mining companies had exported and sold 20,000 tons of copper "for his benefit." He also alleged that an unknown quantity of diamonds and cobalt had been similarly diverted.

Both Republican and Democratic members of the subcommittee posed penetrating questions. Nguza said he agreed with the subcommittee on the danger of the U.S.'s becoming identified with a regime that was destabilizing its own country and on the contamination of U.S. military assistance by corruption and abuse. He denied the suggestion that his allegations were "tribally" or politically motivated, though he acknowledged that he might become a presidential candidate if a more "democratic and liberal system" came into existence.

Asked why he didn't combat large-scale corruption himself when he was prime minister, he claimed he had lacked the power to do so but had encouraged Western countries to pressure Mobutu. Confronted with the view that "the people of Zaire would prefer to tolerate the present conditions rather than risking anarchy or chaos," he rejoined, "The people don't tolerate the situation. You cannot tolerate starvation and misery . . . if there is one thing working very well in Zaire it is the security police."[31]

The Zairian press agency promptly denounced Nguza's "treason." It further informed its readers that among "a certain Weizman" who had been "rector" (!) of the University of Kisangani and expelled from Zaire for subversion, Congressman Solarz, and Belgian business circles, there were "complex and subtle relations" that produced "vociferous hostility" to Zaire.[32]

In Washington, the press gave unusual attention to Nguza's views. In addition, he met with several influential members of Congress, including Paul Tsongas (D-MA), the ranking Democrat on the Senate Africa Subcommittee.

Undaunted, the Reagan administration proposed to double U.S. military aid to $20 million in the coming fiscal year. During a subcommittee hearing, Georgetown University Professor Stephen Cohen, who had been the Carter administration's deputy assistant secretary of state for human rights, recounted interviews he had conducted with Zairians and U.S. and Western officials during two extended trips to the country. He had little doubt that the majority of people detested the regime and perceived the U.S. as Mobutu's main external supporter. Cohen quoted American, Belgian, and other international officials to the effect that no progress had been made in curbing massive diversions of foreign exchange and reforming the military. The subcommittee again voted unanimously to reduce the military request to $4 million.[33]

The recommendation was approved by the full committee on May 11, 1982, with little Republican opposition. Steve Solarz cited Nguza's testimony about how "President Mobutu was diverting literally hundreds of millions of dollars of the limited foreign exchange" and accused the Zaire government of "having literally nothing to show" for hundreds of millions in American military aid over the last twenty years." Chairman Zablocki stated that because of the administration's previous disregard of congressional legislation on Zaire, the entire House aid bill was now in a form that made it impossible to be waived by the president, even in an emergency.[34]

The following day, President Mobutu publicly declared that he was renouncing all American aid. According to Zaire's press agency, his action was in response to "insulting remarks recently made by some American officials" that U.S. aid had been embezzled. The agency attributed Washington's "intolerable attitude" to "American Congressmen of the Democratic Party, especially Steven Solarz" whose Foreign Affairs Committee included two university teachers "who were expelled from Zaire for subversion." (Me and my clone?) It took note of an "anti-Zaire lobby" with "influence" in the committee representing persons dissatisfied with a recent Zaire government decision to sell its diamonds outside of the "traditional networks."[35]

Such a lobby was invisible to me. Perhaps the accusation was aimed at a large Democratic election campaign contributor, Maurice Tempelsman. He held major interests in diamond marketing and had long been close to Mobutu, at times serving as his intermediary with American officials. Zaire had recently shifted its diamond trade away from the South African De Beers monopoly, with which Tempelsman had long been associated.

Two days later, Mobutu announced that he was reestablishing diplomatic relations with Israel, the U.S.'s closest friend in the Middle East. Zaire would thereby become the first of the two dozen African countries that had severed relations with Israel at the onset of the 1973 War to resume normal diplomatic ties with the Jewish state.

Mobutu's move, I wrote Howard, was "transparently designed to get him off the limb he had created by his intemperate reaction to the aid cuts. If Mobutu can now get congressmen to praise him and restore aid, he can not only get off the limb by accepting U.S. aid, he can also go far toward ending political opposition in the U.S." I was by no means crying "wolf." Steve Solarz represented the most Jewish congressional district in the nation. He often mentioned that the main foreign policy issue for his constituents was not Africa policy but support for Israel. Although Howard's electorate was very different, he was reliably pro-Israel, like most congressional Democrats. Both men were Jewish, as were a few other members of the full committee.

Actually, Howard and I had known for a few months that Mobutu was mulling over recognition of Israel, partly as a strategy for overcoming congressional criticism. During his December 1981 visit to the United States, one of his new, well-paid Hampton-Windsor Corporation lobbyists[36]—a former official of B'nai B'rith's Anti-Defamation League, a leading American Jewish organization—had arranged a private meeting between us and Mobutu. One evening we taxied over to the elegant Jefferson Hotel where Mobutu and his entourage was staying. Conspicuously at the president's side was a longtime Israeli advisor.

Earlier, at a committee tea, Mobutu had mentioned that when Israel completed its planned disengagement from the Egyptian Sinai in March or April, there would no longer be any reason "on the plane of pure logic" for Africa not to resume diplomatic relations with it. But in our private meeting, he was more cautious. He said that if Zaire acted alone, it would have "problems" with certain Arab countries that were providing over $200 million in annual economic assistance. Consequently, Zaire and five other African countries were considering joint recognition. That he had now suddenly decided to move unilaterally, and in direct response to a threatened U.S. aid cut, must have disappointed Israel, as it diminished his potential influence on other African states.

(As I exited the hotel, I met Nancy. She had driven into Washington from our home in Northern Virginia to pick me up. With members of Mobutu's entourage also departing, I suggested that she wait with me to try and get a real life look at Mobutu. Sure enough, the Zairian leader quickly appeared. Since our personal relations had been quite civil during various private meetings despite the Zairian press attacks, I stepped up to him and said, "Mr. President, I would like to introduce you to my wife, Nancy." He smiled and replied, "And I would like to introduce you to my wife." Madame Bobi Mobutu greeted us in turn.)

To manage the new political situation created by recognition, I suggested that Howard avoid sending a private telegram or making a public statement complimenting Mobutu on Zaire's recognition of Israel—which the president's lobbyist was requesting. Mobutu and the Zairian press would undoubtedly exploit such messages to claim Howard was now his supporter.

If Howard felt he had to respond to anticipated Israeli Embassy or Jewish organizations' requests for a statement, I recommended that it also refer to Zaire's problems and be made public so that it could not be distorted by the government. Howard should say that Zaire's new position was constructive but needed to be accompanied by reforms in corruption and human rights abuses "before you will consider any alteration of your position."

Howard agreed and followed through. He also wrote Secretary Haig, urging him to protest Saudi Arabia's new decision to terminate diplomatic relations with Zaire. This course was being urged upon Congress and the administration by the American Israel Public Affairs Committee (AIPAC) a powerful pro-Israel group with 50,000 members, contacts in every congressional district, and influence with key campaign donors. American Jews were the vital core of AIPAC's membership.

With encouragement from both the Reagan administration and the Israeli Embassy, AIPAC proceeded with low-key lobbying to persuade members of Congress to soften their stances on Zaire aid. This was not the kind of major campaign AIPAC conducted on higher priority issues, as indicated by its decision to act indirectly through a hired consultant. Since the House Foreign Affairs Committee had already taken its decisions on aid to Zaire, AIPAC's impact would be measured by what transpired in the Senate Foreign Relations Committee.

Fortunately, that committee had finally availed itself of non-administration expertise on the situation in Zaire. A three-person bipartisan staff group had traveled there the previous August and just distributed an extensive report. Its conclusions were similar to ours, as the following excerpts illustrate:

> Throughout the international community, and by many within Zaire, U.S. assistance efforts have often been interpreted as direct support for Mobutu. Zaire's President has promoted the view that the power of the United States stands behind him. His current drive for enhanced U.S. security assistance arises from the need to give credibility to this claim . . . Moreover, identification with the United States is especially important to Mobutu at a time when other traditional sources of Western assistance appear to be seeking to distance themselves . . .
>
> It is widely accepted that [Mobutu] has managed to amass a legendary personal fortune at the nation's expense . . .
>
> While the nature or timing of future changes cannot be confidently predicted, it is increasingly risky for the United States to expect perpetuation of the [political] status quo . . .
>
> In any event, proposals for increased security assistance to Zaire deserve special scrutiny. Repeated reports of corruption, incompetence and deliberate sabotage in the economy and the military all raise

the issue of whether enhanced assistance can or will be effectively used.

The report revealed that of Zaire's seven originally purchased C-130 military transport planes—the target of most U.S. military aid—only two were now operational. And those were being mainly used for the president's personal travel and businesses rather than for military purposes.[37]

When the Foreign Relations Committee "marked up" its foreign aid bill, Senator Tsongas read out portions of the blockbuster report. Consequently, the Republican-majority committee voted to cut the Republican administration's military aid request from $20 million to $10 million.

It so happened that Chris Chamberlin, a friend of mine and fellow "Africanist" scholar, was Tsongas's personal (as opposed to the committee's) foreign policy advisor. Earlier, I had written him a note encouraging Tsongas to focus on Zaire in the mark-up and referring him to classified U.S. intelligence reports discussing corruption by Mobutu and his cronies.

I also conveyed to Chris an interesting tidbit I had gleaned from a conversation with a longtime, highly reliable State Department source. It seemed that when Mobutu's close relative and major financial intermediary, "Uncle" Litho, had recently died, his son prepared for a possible court battle with Mobutu and other relatives over the estate. In this pursuit, he showed Litho's financial records to a Western lawyer. The documents disclosed that Litho's wealth included approximately $1 billion in bank accounts alone. I later wondered whether my intervention with Chris might have contributed in some measure to Senator Tsongas's effort.

The following year, AIPAC and Zaire's lobbyists mounted another mini campaign in both the House and Senate committees, this time with reduced ambition. Instead of supporting controversial military aid, they backed the administration's proposal for $10 million in new foreign exchange assistance. This was different from traditional "development" aid, which was supposed to benefit the poor majority. During our committee's debate, freshman Republican Ed Zschau (R-CA) offered an amendment to make this request more attractive by tying the funds to Zaire's compliance with an anticipated IMF agreement which included certain economic reforms. Zschau observed that Zaire had already positively responded to IMF pressures by mounting an "anti-corruption campaign." Asking "Why should we care about Zaire?" he specifically emphasized its support for U.S. foreign policy as exemplified by its recognition of Israel.

Only one Democrat, Robert Torricelli (D-NJ), spoke in favor of the amendment. Asserting that the assistance could prevent "difficulties" in procuring supplies of strategic minerals, he continued,

> While we can all cite disappointment with the government in some respects, we must nevertheless remember that in difficult moments in American foreign policy initiatives, the government of Zaire has stood with us and has been dependable. Most notably, as has already been pointed out with the Camp David process and in the courage exhibited in recognizing the state of Israel.

Howard responded, "The only real question this amendment presents is whether members of this body want to be in a position of using American tax dollars to subsidize what is one of the most corrupt systems on the face of the African continent." He quoted recent subcommittee testimony by Professor Young: "Reform has been given a fair trial and our inability to produce any significant improvement politically or economically through constructive engagement is now beyond dispute." He also read from a new report by Erwin Blumenthal, former IMF advisor and principal director of Zaire's Central Bank, whose experiences had brought him to a damning conclusion:

> The corrupted system in Zaire with all its wicked and ugly manifestations, its mismanagement and fraud, will destroy all endeavors of international institutions, of friendly governments and the commercial banks toward rehabilitation and Zaire's recovery.[38]

As the vote on the Zschau amendment approached, the committee was suffused with a bazaar-like atmosphere. AIPAC's consultant had spoken with numerous members and asked some of their campaign contributors who were also AIPAC members to contact them. He made headway with three "pragmatic" Democrats, including Torricelli, Rep. Tom Lantos (D-CA), and Rep. Larry Smith (D-FL). As Howard and I walked past the chairman's office, Smith called out to Howard to "please talk to my contributor" who was on the phone urging increased Zaire aid.

Howard had received similar appeals from some of his own donors. According to a federal Foreign Agent Registration Act disclosure statement, Rep. Torricelli had met with, and taken half a dozen phone calls from, Mobutu's lobbyist, who was a resident of his district and campaign contributor. Just before the vote, one liberal Jewish congressman, pressured by both sides, resolved his conflict by leaving the room. In the end, we managed to prevail, 16–13. But that was only because two Republicans we had not contacted unexpectedly voted with us.[39]

Two years later, Rep. Torricelli offered a public *mea culpa* for his vote:

> I feel under some obligation to speak to members of the committee on this issue since two years ago I offered almost the exact same amendment now being offered. Let it suffice to say that I have seen the errors of my ways. It was a mistake. I offered myself an education on Mr. Mobutu and Mr. Mobutu does not deserve any expanded assistance. . . . The facts are that American assistance to that country is being misused on a grand scale."[40]

Left unmentioned were his numerous communications with Mobutu's and AIPAC's lobbyists that helped lead him astray.

CHAPTER 12

THE "CODEL" AND THE BIG
BLOW-UP IN KINSHASA

In August 1983, Howard headed a congressional delegation to seven African countries, including three days in Zaire. Our contingent contained seven Democratic representatives, among them three Black Caucus members, and the ranking subcommittee Republican Gerald Solomon (R-NY).[41]

The "Codel"—the standard Washington term for congressional delegations who travel together—to Zaire forced me to deal with some of the main challenges I had confronted during the previous four and a half years. These were: our Democratic majority's relations with the Republicans, the State Department's rationalizations for and protectiveness of the Mobutu regime, and foreign government lobbying. And, in one agonizing encounter with Mobutu, it compelled me to confront the reimagining of my experience in Kisangani.

Earlier in the month, at another of the full committee's "teas," President Mobutu had said he was looking forward to the Codel's visit. Anticipating a new IMF agreement to assist in "an economic and financial cleanup," he appealed for further assistance from Zaire's friends, "especially the United States." He brought encouraging news that 115 officials were being prosecuted for corruption and he had granted amnesty to all Congolese prosecuted or pursued for security offenses. "There are no prisoners for political opinions" in Zaire, he assured the committee.

During our visit to Kinshasa, we met with a wide variety of official and non-official Zairians and informed expatriates. In addition to Ambassador Peter Constable and various embassy officers, we saw the president, the prime minister and key cabinet ministers, intelligence chiefs, members of the Legislative Council, labor leaders, clergy from the three major religions (including a Catholic Cardinal), university professors, leading political dissidents, representatives of human rights and humanitarian organizations, and Western businessmen. Members of the Codel also visited the main hospital in Kinshasa and U.S. government-aided fish culture, nutrition, and health projects in the capital and Lower Congo province.

In contrast to President Mobutu's assurances, our conversations highlighted the absence of meaningful economic and political reform. While the anticipated IMF program, if adhered to by the government (a big if, as three of the last four programs had been terminated early for poor performance), promised to improve Zaire's formal macroeconomic position, it failed to acknowledge that the majority of financial resources were not listed in official accounts because they were being corruptly diverted by government officials and their cronies.

For example, Madame Mobutu's private secretary had recently been stopped at Brussels National Airport carrying

$6 million in diamonds. As for the vaunted anti-corruption campaign, it was largely focused upon low-level bureaucrats who were not the main culprits; and there had been few actual prosecutions. Moreover, the IMF program paid no attention to economic distribution. We learned that the average monthly salary of an employed urban Zairian was far below the price of the typical family's food staple, a 50-kilogram bag of manioc. According to USAID, 39 percent of children under five in the capital were below 80 percent of weight for age as were 57 percent in mostly rural Kivu Province.

Concerning human rights, despite the amnesty of about eighty-five political prisoners in May, we learned from the local representative of the International Committee of the Red Cross that at least ten new ones had been seized by the time of our visit. More importantly, the internal security apparatus continued to enforce political conformity through secret detentions, torture, and intimidation. The Red Cross had extremely limited access to these security facilities. Further, Western observers confirmed that the Zairian army continued to extort money and services from the population on a massive scale and that U.S. military aid was misused to support generals' private businesses.

But it was the Codel's meeting with ten critics of the government, and its violent aftermath, that provided us with a searing personal experience of the limits of reform.

From our exchanges with a variety of non-governmental actors in Kinshasa, as well as credible press reports, we gathered that the opposition "Group of 13," despite its predominant ethnic Luba component, might enjoy substantial popular support. Nevertheless, in deference to the regime, the

U.S. ambassador forbade his political officers from speaking with them.

Here is the background. In December 1980, thirteen parliamentarians, all members of the sole legal political party, wrote an open letter to President Mobutu. They skewered a wide range of government policies and called for the nonviolent realization of the regime's original democratic promises. (Individual Group of 13 members had emerged as critics of government corruption during the short-lived period of Western-sponsored liberalization following two nearly successful invasions by exiled rebels.) The government responded harshly. It got the legislature to lift the authors' parliamentary immunity, suspended their civil and political rights, and deported them, without their families, to their designated "home villages," where they were placed under surveillance. There was not even the semblance of a judicial process.

Released a year later, they entered negotiations with high government officials, with the goal of establishing a second party, the Union of Democracy and Social Progress (UDPS). Soon they were again arrested, judged, sentenced to fifteen years' imprisonment for conspiracy to destroy the single-party Zaire Constitution and consigned to prisons throughout the country. Liberated under the latest amnesty, they continued to strive for at least *de facto* recognition of a plurality of political opinions. They also called for a national roundtable to write a new constitution and the establishment of a transitional government under President Mobutu.

The government was anxious that by merely meeting with the Group of 13 the Codel would be seen by the population as "designating" a second party, although that was not our purpose. So it arranged with the compliant American Embassy for us to conduct separate, individual meetings with four Group members. This seemed to me an inefficient way for us to obtain an understanding of the Group of 13's experiences and objectives. Individual interviews would inevitably result in duplicative information; we would waste scarce time by posing certain questions to less knowledgeable members; and we would fail to obtain a good impression of the Group's dynamic.

At the first scheduled appointment in the InterContinental Hotel, where we were staying, nine Group of 13 members showed up and asked to meet with us jointly. Howard thought this a more productive way to go. Ranking Republican Solomon agreed. He asked the embassy to seek government approval of the change in format, but the embassy replied that the request would take time to process and was unlikely to succeed. Howard then told the group that the embassy opposed a joint meeting and that he was concerned about the consequences they might bear from the government if it went forward. He could offer no guarantees for their safety. Did any of them wish to meet individually? he asked. They all said no, adding that they wanted to be quoted as a group. The meeting then began, with Solomon raising no objection.

All these men were wearing Western suits and ties, an act of civil disobedience, as Zairian males were now required to wear the supposedly more "authentically African" shirtless and tieless *abacost* suit for such formal occasions. They explained that their defiance was meant to underline to us that the Zairian version of the one-party state was more authoritarian than others in Africa.

Under the constitution that Mobutu had pushed through his legislature, Étienne Tshisekedi wa Mulumba explained, all Zairians were, by birth, members of the single party and subject to its discipline. The constitution further specified that Mobutu was that party's "sole organ" of decision-making and that its "guiding doctrine" was "Mobutuism." Thus, no matter what modest powers the single-party legislators theoretically possessed under the constitution, Mobutu could command them as party members to expel dissenters, whom he could then subject to party "discipline" such as internal exile to their impoverished "home villages." That, Tshisekedi stated, was exactly what had happened to them when they had criticized the regime's corruption.

After about an hour, Solomon left the room for a few minutes. Walking back, he looked out a window and noticed a demonstration forming in the vacant lot across from the hotel. Upon returning, he handed Howard a note which read:

> There are about a hundred demonstrators outside and in support of these people. WE HAVE BEEN USED! Either you or I should reinforce that we have met with them as individuals and not as a group or organization. If they try to say anything different it will be necessary to issue a press release contradicting them, which would be embarrassing for them. And I will see to it.

Howard responded by respecting Solomon's concern while trimming its hard edges. He cautioned the ex-parliamentarians that the delegation was concerned that they not publicly state that we met with them as a group or organization rather than as individuals. The meeting then resumed with Solomon's continued participation.

Here was an instructive example of bipartisan collaboration between two representatives, one a passionate liberal and the other a strong conservative, who held contrasting views of Zaire policy. Solomon was anxious to support a friendly government; Wolpe was eager to distance America from an oppressive regime. Nonetheless, they had managed to reach agreement on the productivity of a collective meeting and the concomitant need, as guests of the government, to manage the public perception of the event.

I found the discussion enlightening. To my surprise, members of the Group stated congressional pressure had forced Mobutu to grant them and other political prisoners amnesty. Thanking us, some went as far as saying that without such pressure they would have been killed. They also brought forward concrete examples of major corruption and human rights abuses, rebutted Western fears that without Mobutu the country would succumb to chaos or Communism, and explained that for historical reasons and because the U.S. was the leader of the West, Zairians blamed America more than Belgium and France for Mobutu's actions—even though the latter were currently providing more military assistance.

Toward the end of the meeting, we were informed that the individual who had printed the group members' business cards was under arrest and that a supporter who had been bringing us the Group of 13's formal position paper had also been detained in the hotel elevator.

When our interlocutors departed, we later learned they were greeted by close to 100 sympathizers in the hotel's front parking lot. One ex-parliamentarian was lifted onto the shoulders of supporters who gave a "V for Victory" sign. Three banners welcomed the American delegation, proclaimed "Victory," and carried the name of the desired second party. We sped off to our other appointments, but Congressman Mickey Leland (D-TX) returned to the hotel because he had forgotten his money. In doing so, he became an eyewitness to a horrific scene which he subsequently recounted:

> Several men were wielding large cinder blocks to destroy a car in the parking lot. Standing near me was an American hired by the U.S. Embassy to handle transportation for the delegation's visit. He said that I should ignore what was happening, dismissing it as "typical African behavior." Suddenly people were running in the parking lot and about twenty men emerged from jeep-like vehicles and began to kick and beat several people. I saw one man being whipped by three men. Another was grabbed by two or three men, thrown to the ground, and beaten with what appeared to be chains. I did not understand what was going on or who was being beaten until I noticed one of the victims being yanked by his necktie and slammed to the ground. . . . It was one of the ex-parliamentarians we had just met. Blood was pouring from his forehead and soaking his shirt. I headed down a ramp from the hotel entrance to help him, but the embassy employee grasped me and warned that I might be beaten or killed. I asked him where the police were, and he pointed out a policeman who was watching the beatings without interceding. I

then checked with embassy personnel in the control center set up in the hotel to coordinate the delegation's visit and found that several of them had witnessed the destruction of the automobiles and the beatings. I hurried to the embassy where the American ambassador attempted to dismiss the beatings by characterizing them as behavior which "happens all the time." He told me that this was a different society from ours and I did not understand it. I went back to the hotel where I waited until the rest of the delegation had returned and told them what I had seen. Later we learned that six of those whom we had met with had been beaten and imprisoned.

A few days earlier, during our flight from Washington to Addis Ababa, Ethiopia, Leland had approached me and confided that he didn't want to go to Zaire. He was a strong opponent of Mobutu. I told him that some of our meetings would be with Zairian critics of Mobutu and that the information we acquired on the trip could be useful in persuading Congress to be more skeptical of the regime. Mickey was one of the warmest-hearted congressmen I came to know. I remember him at a feeding station in Ethiopia, where hundreds of people waited in the rain for a food distribution that was several days late, amusing the hungry children by jumping on a mule with his cowboy hat. I was saddened that my words had possibly contributed to bringing him face to face with such violence.

Aware of the incident from Leland's and embassy officers' reports, the ambassador called the Foreign Ministry to express his and the Codel's shock and urged the government to promptly "correct" the situation. Later that evening, a half dozen imprisoned ex-parliamentarians were released. Before that, the congressmen, after caucusing among themselves and meeting with the ambassador, had decided to send a strong letter to President Mobutu protesting the beatings and detentions. It demanded the immediate release of, and a meeting with, those arrested, a report on "how this tragic event occurred," a report on the physical condition of those arrested and injured, and a guarantee that no further action would be taken against those individuals and their families as a result of this incident. Separately, the Codel decided to decline a scheduled luncheon meeting with Mobutu aboard his yacht the following day. Instead, they proposed to see him elsewhere for "a working session."

Ambassador Constable strongly opposed these decisions. He warned the delegation that it was "asking for a confrontation," "prejudging" the government's responsibility without "full knowledge of the facts," and "appeared to be suggesting that the president was personally responsible." Rejecting the president's invitation to lunch was "insulting" and "unprecedented" and risked his refusing to meet with them at all.

Nevertheless, the congressmen were determined to send their letter. In a gesture to the ambassador, they decided they would meet Mobutu on his boat but decline lunch: it would be unseemly to engage in a festive social event as if nothing terrible had just happened. Solomon proposed that the Codel offer a "diplomatic" excuse for not eating—that some of its members had gotten sick from food consumed in Ethiopia— but the ambassador doubted that would be convincing.

The next afternoon we boarded the Kamanyola, a former Congo riverboat that had once plied the thousand miles from Kinshasa to Kisangani. With its steamer removed, it was now the president's personal yacht. The vessel was enormous and well-appointed. It had three decks, a helipad, and sonar and other communications facilities. There were three VIP bedrooms and cabins and a dormitory for staff. Soon after we left port, there was a deafening noise. We were quickly ushered outside to watch the president's helicopter land.

Unaccustomed to being turned down for lunch, the President seated us at tables in the sixty-seat dining room on the second deck. He appeared to be coaxing the members to reconsider their lunch boycott. It was almost touching how he tempted them—in vain—by sending waiters around with hors d'oeuvres and offering "pineapple juice from my own farm." After a while, we got down to business.

In a lounge toward the rear of the boat, our delegation was seated on a bench on one side of the president and his interpreter. On the opposite bench sat the foreign minister and a presidential advisor. To my shock and dismay, Mobutu began the conversation by launching an attack upon me, something he had never done in any of our previous private meetings.

For several minutes he repeated the accusations that had been lodged against me in Kisangani twelve years earlier, ones which his government had subsequently dropped. He even criticized expert testimony I had given to Senate and House committees back in 1976 and 1977. (His Belgian friend, diplomat Alfred Cahen, once told me, "He reads everything.") In Mobutu's view, I had sinned by falsely predicting his eventual overthrow.

As he proceeded, I worried that one or more members of our delegation would be influenced by his effort to discredit me and that the attack was diverting attention from the broader political issues at hand. I was at a loss as to how I could effectively and respectfully reply if one of our members requested it. Happily, no one in our delegation stirred and I never heard anything more about it—even from Howard. I still wonder if the low voice of the interpreter or the fact that the president's remarks were extraneous to the immediate crisis saved me. I was grateful that the American embassy officer present did not recount this portion of Mobutu's discussion in his report. That might have rekindled the annoying Foreign Service Officer gossip about my "troublemaking" in Kisangani, "fake news" I had been trying to leave behind.

As the meeting continued, Mobutu angrily accused the Codel of meeting the ex-parliamentarians as a group, pointing out that this was a flagrant violation of the law and constitution since we had thereby "designated" a second political party. He regretted that our visit had been marred by the "stupid" incident of beatings which were carried out, he claimed, by "party youth" provoked by the "illegal" demonstration in front of the hotel. He promised that these young people would be hauled before the party's disciplinary committee. He denied any responsibility for the incident, noting that it had taken place while he was touring Kinshasa following his return that afternoon from Europe and America.

Dwelling on the opposition demonstration, he repeatedly remarked, "Their signs said 'Victory.' Victory over whom?" What part of this, I wondered, was political anxiety and what part pure egotism? Against the thrust of our other interviews, he dismissed the Group of 13 as having no popular support. As for the individual arrested in the elevator, Bossassi Epole, he was a "Communist sympathizer" being held in forty-eight-hour detention.

In a softer vein, he assured us that we were free to meet with Bossassi as well as the detainees released the previous evening, and there would be no reprisals against the Group of 13 for the incident. He promised to respond to the delegation's letter, but only regarding "points that merit a reply."

Since the dramatic events of the previous day had exposed the central political problem in Zaire, making it the prime topic of our conversation, Mobutu was left with little time to lobby us on other matters. Concerning human rights, he denied, "on my honor as Chief of State and a soldier," the report we had received the evening before from the Red Cross delegate that there were at least ten new political prisoners since the May amnesty. He insisted he had kept "my pledge to the House Foreign Affairs Committee" days earlier that "there are no political prisoners in Zaire." He emphasized that the IMF and World Bank liked his new economic reform program. And since no U.S. aid went directly into the Zaire government's treasury, it should not be "singled out" for reductions.

Howard led off the delegation's response by complimenting Mobutu on various foreign policy initiatives: reconciliation with neighboring Angola, dispatching troops to Chad to oppose Libyan expansionism, and diplomatic recognition of Israel. Still, he remonstrated, the right of free people to assemble peacefully had been violated and the incident had confirmed widespread allegations of a troubled human rights environment in Zaire. Alongside the history of government corruption and economic mismanagement, the latest affair made it more difficult for members of Congress to justify increased aid to Zaire to their constituents. Mobutu admonished Howard for always dwelling on past events and not recognizing the positive steps he had taken.

Congressman Solomon spoke next. He declared himself a strong supporter of Zaire who had "carried the ball" for that nation in Congress. He added that he was also a strong backer of President Reagan, whom he knew to be a close friend of Zaire. Solomon thanked President Mobutu for his support of American policies in the United Nations and Central America, sending troops to Chad, and recognizing Israel. Nevertheless, he deplored the "unnecessary" and "vicious" violence which had occurred at the hotel. If the ex-parliamentarians had broken Zairian law, he remarked, "they should have been led away in handcuffs, not beaten."

Approaching this traumatic episode from two different perspectives, the liberal Democrat and conservative Republican had arrived at similar conclusions about the unacceptability of what had happened and the need to confront the president directly about it.

Other members of the delegation spoke in like terms, adding their individual takes. Congressman Ted Weiss (D-NY) said he had come to Zaire with an open mind and been impressed by Mobutu's words at the committee tea. But he had been shocked by the incident at the hotel. While he did not believe the president was personally responsible, he thought there was a "strong possibility" that Mobutu's support of human rights had not permeated down to other elements of his government. Mickey Leland began by noting he was vice-chairman of the

Congressional Black Caucus and deeply concerned about human rights. Consequently, he had been "profoundly disturbed" by the violence. Coming from a society where he was free to criticize his president, he said he had come here feeling free to criticize the president of Zaire.

Mobutu interrupted sharply, "You go too far."

As the meeting ended, Mobutu sourly observed that he had repeatedly expressed his regrets and embarrassment concerning the incident, but "that apparently means nothing to you."

I admit I was a bit unnerved by the president's attack on me. Having learned something about risk-taking from my first sojourn in Zaire, in advance of the trip I had asked the State Department to determine whether there were any risks to my personal security, given that I had been previously denounced in public statements by Mobutu and his press agency.

The embassy replied, "Although you are regarded in the government of Zaire as a hostile critic of the regime, the government of Zaire will take all appropriate steps to assure that you are treated with the same courtesy and regard for your safety as all other members of the Codel." Nonetheless, that night in my hotel room, I hungrily debated whether I should order a ham and cheese sandwich—the only sandwich available—from room service, just in case it was poisoned! Many members of the Zairian "political class" believed that Mobutu and other Zairians used poison on their enemies. On the other hand, even if the president possessed a difficult-to-trace poison, it would be pretty suspicious if a staff member of a Congressional delegation expired shortly after being castigated by him. Once again, I faced a difficult choice in the Congo. I ordered the sandwich and, after a pause, consumed it with no untoward consequences.

The next day, several members of the Group of 13, accompanied by three supporters, met us again at the hotel. It was depressing to see these gentlemen who had sat with us in their suits and ties and patiently articulated their political positions a day earlier, standing before us now, coatless and tieless, with their heads and faces horribly cut, swollen, and bandaged. In subdued tones, five released dissidents related that they had been attacked not by a "youth group," as Mobutu maintained, but by the President's Special Brigade, a claim soon confirmed by the embassy.

As the small demonstration was dispersing, they said, they had been assaulted by soldiers in civilian dress with metal-studded military belts and bayonets. They were beaten, some into unconsciousness, and transported to a secret police prison in the Colonel Tshatshi Military Camp in the OAU Village section of Kinshasa, where President Mobutu lived. There they were attacked again with truncheons. Some were left nude on the ground. Up to fifty of their supporters and innocent passersby were said to have been arrested and beaten.

Their accounts, broadly confirmed by the embassy, undermined Mobutu's disclaimer of responsibility. The Presidential Brigade was the military unit closest to Mobutu, the one most familiar with his expectations. It was implausible to think that the brigade would not have been in communication with him as he arrived at the airport from abroad and toured Kinshasa while a pro-second party demonstration was taking place outside the hotel where the Codel was meeting with the opposition. Moreover, the detainees had been imprisoned for hours not far from Mobutu's residence

Ex- parliamentarian and Group of 13 member Lusanga Ngiele one day after arrest and beating by President Mobutu's Special Brigade, August 12, 1983.

and released only after the Embassy had relayed its "shock" and called for corrections.

One of the sadder moments of my life was when I asked some of these dignified men to strip down to their underwear so the U.S. Army doctor accompanying our delegation could record their injuries. Howard and Solomon had asked Ambassador Constable, who oversaw all U.S. agency personnel in the country, to permit the doctor to conduct the examinations. After some discussion, he had refused, authorizing the doctor only to administer first aid to those requesting it. He claimed that "a detailed medical report on the wounds sustained was beyond the expertise and the mandate of both the doctor and the delegation" and questioned "the propriety of the Codel conducting a quasi-judicial examination of the victims." Why, I wondered, was he going to such extremes to protect the image of this client regime?

While the ambassador was pondering the issue, the doctor had managed to examine three individuals. Meanwhile, Congressman's Solomon's minority staff aide, David Lonie, and I began recording the visible injuries to three others whom we interviewed in the adjoining bathroom. Our combined inquiries revealed contusions, sutured lacerations, severe swellings and bruises, a clinically fractured rib (according to the doctor), a frightening looking facial edema, and numerous marked discolorations of the head, chest, legs, back, and buttocks. In his subsequent written report, the doctor curtly concluded that the injuries to the three people he examined "do not appear to be life, limb, or vision threatening but will be painful."

Next, the Codel met with Bossassi, the UDPS supporter and alleged Communist sympathizer who had been arrested in the hotel elevator. He was brought to us escorted by the head of the security police and the CIA station chief. The sight of the latter, a beefy fellow, leading the slight, younger man to his chair, brought back disturbing memories of past CIA activities in the Congo.

Appearing to speak freely after the intelligence officials left the room, Bossassi said he had not been physically tortured—"They were probably afraid you would see me"—but had been interrogated from 8 p.m. until 10 a.m. in a cell "without light and air. . . . They had tried psychological means to get me to change my mind." He recounted having been a supporter of Mobutu as a party youth official at his university before becoming disillusioned and going into exile in Europe for thirteen years.

Returning to the country in 1980, he said he had become an advisor to the government's National Security Committee to assist with projected party reforms. But several months ago he had been arrested for his "critical opinions," then tortured, including by electroshocks, in prison. Released under the amnesty, he had worked with the Group of 13 to produce the position paper he was carrying to us when he was detained. Under rigorous questioning by Solomon, he denied that he was a Communist sympathizer, professing to believe in non-collective, non-Marxist Socialism. He maintained that he was not seeking to change Zaire's economic system or exclude American capital, but to "preserve democracy." Howard told him that we had requested he not be harassed after his expected release. Near the end of the discussion, Congresswoman Katie Hall (D-OH) asked him, "What do you expect?" He answered, "Anything . . . when you leave I'm still here and expect everything." Bossassi and the Group of 13's printer would remain in detention for another four months.

The Codel's next stop was Zimbabwe, but we arranged to return to Kinshasa's N'djili Airport for refueling and to check on the welfare of the Group of 13. When we landed, the ambassador came aboard and suggested a plan to help ensure the dissidents would remain at liberty. The Codel would urgently send messages to each individual in the Group, stating that its interest in the Group's well-being "does not extend to . . . support for their political activities" or include "efforts to protect them from arrest for activities in violation of the Zairian Constitution or the laws of the country." In addition, any public statement by the Codel on its Kinshasa visit should reference this warning. The delegation unanimously rejected the ambassador's request, which appeared to constitute a blank check for indiscriminate political repression.

During our visit, it had become evident to many of us that the embassy's strong impulse to protect the Zairian regime was causing it to shade the truth. How this disposition distorted its reporting to Washington became even clearer to me when we received, during the latter part of our Africa trip, the embassy's cables to Washington regarding our visit. Working closely with David, I drafted an eight-page cable to State that was edited and approved by both Wolpe and Solomon. It criticized major omissions in the embassy's reports that "significantly alter picture CODEL saw of Zaire."[42]

We mentioned several outstanding points missing from the embassy's report on our meeting with the Group of 13. These included the Codel's agreement that it was logical, given time constraints and the Group's preference, to meet with individual members at the same time; the Group's discussion of how the Zairian system aspired to be more authoritarian than those of other one-party African states; its description of its members' year-long internal exile and subsequent negotiations with the government over its proposed second party; its reference to a confidential internal ministry of finance report describing large-scale embezzlement of government funds by Mobutu; its appeal for U.S. assistance to be tied to "respect for pluralism" and "ordered, negotiated reform"; and its desire that U.S. humanitarian aid be provided via private, nongovernmental agencies rather than the Zaire government.

The embassy's account of our discussion with Mobutu was also inadequate. It understated Mobutu's anger and his conviction that the delegation, by simply meeting with members of the Group, was "designating" a second party. It missed the insecurity or egotism manifested in his discussion of the demonstration outside the hotel.

The embassy had made no effort to discuss with us various informal conversations we conducted at receptions and elsewhere with Zairians in and out of the government. These contradicted Mobutu's claims that there were no political prisoners and the Group of 13 had no support. Along with some of our formal interviews, they challenged the embassy's contention, in its initial briefing of the Codel, that there was "no great hostility from the population" to the government.

Finally, the embassy's account of the Bossassi meeting failed to mention his depictions of his current "psychological" interrogation and earlier physical torture, professed support for U.S. principles of democracy and denial of ever having been party to Communism.

In sum, the embassy's reports deprived the State Department of important information regarding both the opposition and the Mobutu government.

While sometimes depressing, this short, intense visit aided my evolution into a more mature political actor. Formerly, I saw our subcommittee's major goal in Zaire rather mechanically. If we reduced the administration's request for military aid to Mobutu, informed Zairians would spread the word that the U.S. was distancing itself somewhat from the corrupt and repressive regime. On the ground, I learned that the process was subtler. Not just our aid cuts, but our public expressions of the reasons behind them had resonated with both Mobutu and his opponents. Moreover, in limited ways our actions were already benefiting individual lives. For example, it became clearer from our various discussions that Mobutu was using the new political amnesty to gain favor with Congress.

Those three days also provided me with new insights into the obstacles that Howard and I had been struggling against and how we might better approach them. A continuing problem had been our relationship with the Republicans. Previously, I had felt most comfortable simply putting forward my analysis of a situation and waiting for the minority to engage. But during this trip, Howard and I proactively sought ways to work with Solomon and David. Without either side abandoning its perspective on overall Zaire policy, we were able to forge common positions toward the government's attempt to minimize the Codel's contact with the opposition and use violence against them. And we jointly resisted the embassy's zeal to protect its client regime, no matter what it did.

This cooperation had legs. Six months later, the subcommittee met to mark up a new foreign aid bill. Solomon "reluctantly" accepted the majority's renewed recommendation for a $4 million ceiling on military aid to Zaire as part of a broad compromise involving military assistance to several African states. "If you recall last year," he observed, "we had so many differences and I think it even created some hard feelings. But this truly has been a bipartisan effort . . . your staff in particular has been outstanding in this cooperation and I really appreciate it."[43]

Prior to the trip, we had spent years confronting Washington policy makers' defensiveness on Zaire, their tendency to give their client regime the benefit of the doubt. Even so, I had not anticipated the degree to which the American Embassy under President Reagan and Assistant Secretary of State for African Affairs Chester Crocker would try to manipulate Congress's perceptions of regime abuses. Nor had I contemplated that it would dispatch half-truthful cables on what transpired in our meetings to the State Department. While we had little hope of overturning these practices, we had decided to send our own cable to State to set the record straight in Washington and hopefully deter the State Department from incorporating the embassy's distortions of political reality into its future legislative appearances.

My perspective on foreign lobbying also deepened. The private and public interventions of the Zaire government's lobbyists had been a recurring problem for us, especially when supplemented by the pleadings of domestic special interests. In this circumstance however, the foreign lobbyist was President Mobutu himself. While that might seem advantageous for him considering his stature and knowledge and that he was operating on home ground, his techniques proved highly counterproductive. He obviously lied to us about who was responsible for the beatings and arrests of members and supporters of the Group of 13. And accusing members of Congress of provoking the incident was not the way a good professional lobbyist would have begun a conversation aimed at alleviating legislative opposition.

From his exalted position, Mobutu never seemed to appreciate how deeply affected the delegation had been by what he called a "stupid" and "embarrassing" act of political repression. Nor did he appear to understand that his public confrontation with the Codel—there was abundant press coverage—was aiding our strategy of distancing the U.S. from his regime in the eyes of his people.

Finally, against my inveterate rationalism and academic impulse to respond to criticism, I recognized the wisdom of silence when Mobutu tried to discredit me. I would never change his mind about what had happened in Kisangani. And it would have been virtually impossible to have provided the Codel with a simple refutation on the spot. Previously, when State Department officials gossiped that I was seeking revenge for a bad experience in Kisangani by "poisoning the well" in Congress, I had chafed at Howard's injunction to move on rather than prolong the conversation. Now I had come to appreciate his judgment that it was unnecessary and unproductive to respond to personal attacks that were invisible to the broader public.

Less than four months after our departure, the government again detained Group of 13 members and hundreds of their supporters. Once more, the leaders were relegated to their "ancestral villages." Most had never actually lived in these places, which were mainly associated with their parents. This time their family members were forced to join them, abandoning their urban schools and jobs. From letters members of the Group smuggled out to Howard, other members of our delegation, and Steve Solarz, as well as reports by Amnesty International, we learned that they were deprived of adequate food, clothing, medical care and medicines, schooling, work and housing. Sometimes they were even prevented from having social relations with others in their villages.

Over the next few years, Howard and other members sent communications to high State Department officials, asking them to intervene with the Zaire government to ameliorate these inhuman conditions. Disappointingly, these pleas produced minimal responses. There were only a few modest improvements on the ground. In mid-1985, the opposition leaders were again released. Steve, who had rejoined the subcommittee, had dinner with them in Kinshasa. But they were soon detained again. During their various confinements most members of the Group suffered from serious, untreated illnesses.

A leading figure was Makanda Mpinga. In March 1985, he wrote Howard a letter which was transmitted to us by the American Embassy. It reported that he and two other Group of 13 members had been removed from their villages after an outbreak of violence between their supporters and security forces. "I am detained at Kamina [a military base] isolated in a villa abandoned for 25 years—without doors or windows but in a marshland," he wrote. "Medical care, I have not always had it, but in addition I find myself brutally isolated now without medicine or care and especially without food. . . . I am seriously ill. It's since November 1983 that I have implored for authorization to be visited by a doctor and I have not obtained this." Makanda composed his letter on both sides of a small brown Zambia Sugar Company bag "to show you in what situation we find ourselves."

After Howard and other members of the Codel sent Assistant Secretary Crocker a new letter requesting their urgent intervention in favor of more humane treatment of Makanda and others, Group members were released, but, as usual, re-arrested a few months later. In November 1986, members of the Codel complained to Crocker about their harsh conditions of detention. He replied that Makanda had been brought to a hospital "at government expense" (!) and Tshisekedi had requested similar treatment for "chronic health problems." On March 6, 1987, Makanda died at a hospital in Belgium, where he had been transferred after a long delay.

Following extreme Zaire government pressure on their living conditions, the Group's leaders agreed, in mid-1987, to a conditional release from imprisonment. The president would reintegrate them into the single party, but they would enjoy "the right to have alternative political leanings." How this would work in practice was unclear. And many pro-UDPS militants remained in jail.

~~~

CHAPTER 13

MOBUTU AND COMPANY PURSUE THE CONGRESSIONAL BLACK CAUCUS

By 1987, due to a mix of Foreign Affairs and Appropriations Committee actions and the executive branch's need to ration scarce worldwide security assistance funds, U.S. military aid to Zaire had descended to $3 million a year and there were no longer any funds for non-developmental foreign exchange support. While our subcommittee lacked the political force to fully disassociate the U.S. aid program from the Mobutu government's abuses, it had noticeably deflated the political symbolism of American support.

Two new lobbying forces now took shape. One was the Rainbow Lobby, a subsidiary of the leftist New Alliance Party that had previously concentrated on advocating for ballot access for third parties.[44] Supported largely by small donations obtained from door-to-door canvassing, it latched on to the Zaire issue after being approached by a Zairian exile. It framed its involvement as extending its thrust for democratization and confronting U.S. support for "apartheid's key ally" in Southern African conflicts. (Mobutu had long assisted South African-aided guerillas in neighboring Angola.)

Over the summer, the Lobby persuaded Rep. Ron Dellums (D-CA), a leading left-liberal member of the Congressional Black Caucus, to introduce a bill prohibiting U.S. security assistance and providing developmental and food assistance to the maximum feasible extent through private and voluntary organizations rather than the government. The legislation met Dellums's desire to further validate his leadership in the congressional movement to sanction the White minority regime in South Africa by demonstrating an equal willingness to penalize a Black tyranny. By September, sixteen of the twenty-three members of the Congressional Black Caucus had signed on as co-sponsors.

In November, the Lobby brought Group of 13 leader Tshisekedi to Washington where they arranged meetings with several members of Congress. One of those impressed was Rep. Robert Mrazek (D-NY), a member of the key House Appropriations Foreign Operations Subcommittee, who wanted to become more involved in human rights issues. Two months later, in response to reports that Tshisekedi and many of his supporters had been arrested and beaten for trying to hold a peaceful public meeting, he organized a letter of protest to President Mobutu that was signed by forty-eight congresspersons, including eight members of the Black Caucus. It warned, "It is difficult for Members of the United States Congress to continue sending U.S. military and economic aid in light of current political conditions."

While the Rainbow Lobby's parent New Alliance Party had a significant following among voters in New York State, it was quite controversial. Some former members had gone so far as to accuse it of being a manipulative cult-like group built around its leader, Fred Newman. Newman ran several psychology clinics based on his own brand of "social therapy." He was attacked by B'nai B'rith's Anti-Defamation League for past statements that American Jews had made a "deal with the devil" to protect themselves from another Holocaust by functioning as "stormtroopers of decadent capitalism against people of color the world over." Whatever the truth about the Alliance, the two individuals I came to know best in the Rainbow Lobby's Zaire campaign—one a skilled lobbyist and the other a crack reporter for the Alliance newspaper—were well-informed, proficient, and personable.

I appreciated the advent of an outside ally working the halls of Congress and regularly exchanged information with the Lobby. Over the years, Howard and I had received numerous supportive letters from returned Peace Corps volunteers, American missionaries working in Zaire, and Congolese exiles, many of whom provided important insights into the political situation. We had also followed closely the valuable reports of Amnesty International and other international groups concerning human rights abuses.

Yet before the arrival of the Rainbow Lobby, there had been no U.S. citizens' organization concerned with human rights and democracy lobbying Congress to take positions on U.S. aid to Zaire. With multiple African issues on the subcommittee's plate and a small staff, our own outreach to Congress had been largely limited to members of the authorizing and appropriating committees.

One day, the New Alliance reporter came to my office and asked if I'd heard that Congressman Leland had gone fishing with Mobutu. I stared at him in disbelief. Even before Mickey had witnessed the beatings of the ex-parliamentarians, his distaste for the Mobutu regime had been so intense that he had questioned our plan to visit Zaire. Yet a major Kinshasa newspaper was reporting that during a recent visit to the country he had stated, "I am impressed by the attitude of President Mobutu. Henceforth I will be his supporter in front of the U.S. Congress." As the outgoing head of the Black Caucus, Leland had even invited Mobutu to address its annual meeting. In a tape-recorded conversation between Tshisekedi and Leland that the reporter shared with me, Mickey emphasized that he went to talk to Mobutu about hunger (he was now chair of the House Select Committee on Hunger), AIDS, and population growth, but added significantly, "If I've got to talk to the devil to achieve some change [in Zaire], I'm going to do that."

At my suggestion, Howard met with Mickey. The latter frankly explained that he had gone to Zaire to see Mobutu at the urging of a wealthy, Democratic party-connected businessman named Grover Connell. Connell was chairman of Connell Rice & Sugar, a leading commodities firm that had sold rice to Zaire in the past and had recently signed a new contract with the government. Between 1986 and 1988, Leland received $6,000 in "honoraria" for three visits to the company to discuss legislative developments with its executives. Connell and his wife also contributed $2,000 to Leland's 1988 campaign.[45]

The rewards for Connell's lobbying effort were underlined three months after Leland's visit. His company became the exclusive purchasing agent for certain U.S. supplies for Zaire's giant state mining corporation, Gécamines. The deal was facilitated by Mobutu's son Manda, who the U.S. Embassy learned had received at least $2 million from Connell. Gécamines was later forced to cancel the contract under pressure from Zaire's World Bank financiers who were concerned about "excessive fees paid to agents."[46]

Howard enjoyed a close political and personal relationship with Mickey. The two had worked together to triple U.S. food aid to Africa during the severe mid-1980s drought. Howard let him know how he felt about his apparent turnabout. In response, Howard told me, Mickey "minimized the significance of the interaction that had occurred." It is true that Mickey subsequently did nothing noticeable, legislatively, or otherwise, to advance Mobutu's cause. On the other hand, he declined to co-sponsor Dellums's bill. (In August 1989, Mickey, along with members of his staff, other Americans and Ethiopians, tragically died in a plane crash as they attempted to fly in bad weather to a refugee camp for Sudanese boys.)

The incoming chairman of the Black Caucus was Rep. Mervyn Dymally (D-CA).[47] Having initially agreed to Leland's request to host Mobutu, Dymally disinvited him when opposition developed within the caucus and among some of its outside supporters. Nevertheless, Dymally met with Mobutu in New York City where, he later said, they discussed human rights.

Thus began Mobutu's second lobbying initiative aimed at corralling the Black Caucus. This one would also be pushed by a businessman financially dependent upon the Zairian president. In January 1988, Dymally spent ten days in Zaire as Mobutu's guest. After Rep. Mrazek's congressional letter protesting the violent suppression of Tshisekedi's political meeting, Dymally wrote Mrazek that he had discussed the matter with Mobutu. The president had pointed out to him that the incident had nothing to do with politics but was provoked by the violation of a local ordnance against demonstrating without a permit. Dymally also challenged Amnesty International, State Department, and press estimates of the human toll of the incident.

At Dymally's suggestion, the Zairian-American Research Institute (ZARI) was incorporated in Washington, D.C., "to improve friendship, cooperation and improved relations between Zaire and the United States." Two of its three directors were former staff aides or associates of the congressman. In September 1988, Dymally and ZARI issued simultaneous press releases asserting that the congressman, through his meetings with Mobutu in Europe and Zaire, had succeeded in "his seven-month ongoing human rights plea" for Tshisekedi's release. Dymally praised Mobutu's decision as "an effort to show there is room for divergent opinions within Zaire." However, Tshisekedi himself refused to credit Dymally for Mobutu's action. U.S. Ambassador to Zaire Bill Harrop subsequently told me, "Dymally really didn't have anything to do with Tshisekedi's release. Mobutu used his visit." Within five months, Tshisekedi was again detained, and he remained under house arrest for more than a year afterward.

Like Leland, Dymally declined to endorse the Dellums bill, seeking instead "to keep a dialogue open" with Mobutu. Meanwhile, ZARI financed trips by a few black mayors and congressmen to Zaire. But this program got some bad publicity when Rep. Gus Savage (D-IL) was accused of sexually assaulting a female Peace Corps volunteer who had briefed him on the agency's country program. Savage too spurned Dellums's legislation.

I was surprised by Dymally's moves. I had briefed him once on African issues and found him well-informed. As a generally liberal member of the Foreign Affairs Committee he had voted our way on Zaire and publicly criticized the Mobutu regime. For example, during a 1983 full committee meeting he had devastatingly inquired of a State Department representative who had praised Mobutu's new anti-corruption initiative, "Would you just explain to me how does the chief honcho of corruption institute reforms?"[48]

What accounted for the congressman's turnabout? He later told me that it was the result of his personal and political relationship (including a $2,500 contribution to his 1988 campaign) with an African-born American businessman. He was "fascinated," he recalled, by Mamadi Diane, a Muslim "like my father." He thought that he would not have gone to Zaire at all and "probably would never have been involved in the issue" had Diane not pressed him to "see it for yourself."

Like Connell, Diane was enmeshed in Mobutu's financial orbit. He had recently become the Zaire government's agent for the U.S. government's food assistance program, receiving 2.5 percent of the shipping costs under a contract that was renewable annually. He was reportedly "in business" with a member of Mobutu's inner circle, businessman Bemba Saloana. The latter provided much of the funding for ZARI, of which Diane was president.[49]

Dymally was not above using his budding relationship with Mobutu for his own political purposes. At the congressman's request, the Zairian leader contributed $250,000 to a charity run by Dick Griffey, a prominent Los Angeles African American businessman and Dymally supporter. (Dymally represented a close suburb of Los Angeles.) The organization was producing and marketing a telethon on conditions in Southern Africa, including an appeal for funds to help African children. Griffey contributed $1,750 to Dymally's 1988 campaign, with an additional $2,000 being provided by employees of his company, Solar Records. Beyond these contributions, Dymally told me that he admired Griffey "because he was the only Black with a five-story building in Hollywood" and possessed a vision of "economic empowerment" for Africa.[50]

Knowing that our subcommittee's progress in distancing the U.S. from the regime was incomplete and still tenuous, I was concerned about Leland's and Dymally's initiatives. In retrospect, my fears proved excessive. Leland did Connell a favor, but largely folded his cards after Howard approached him. The Rainbow Lobby's work on the Dellums bill had provided a focal point for mobilizing the main body of the Black Caucus and involving Rep. Mrazek, a key figure on the relevant Appropriations Subcommittee.

And Howard's strong relationship with both Dellums and the Black Caucus, forged through years of collaboration on legislation sanctioning White-ruled regimes in Southern Africa, would almost certainly have forestalled major Caucus defections.

Finally, Dymally was not a particularly influential member of the Foreign Affairs Committee. And in the end, his staying power was limited. He joined the Africa Subcommittee in 1989, participating actively in our hearings and discussions.

But he made no effort to alter Howard's recommendations on aid to Zaire. His only comment on the subject at our mark-up of legislation was a defensive one: "I was criticized by the left for going to Zaire," but it was "our obligation as African Americans . . . to open up a dialogue with African leadership even in areas where we have major disagreements."[51]

The Leland-Dymally pattern of doing something to gratify their pro-Mobutu benefactors but not following through with meaningful action extended to other members of Congress. Connell sponsored two Washington, D.C., receptions for Mobutu in 1988 and 1989, each of which attracted about fifty members.

As a major contributor to the Democratic Party and Democratic campaigns who also distributed $347,000 in honoraria to congressmen from 1986 to 1989, Connell had a wide acquaintance with members. In January 1990, he personally shepherded four congressmen to Zaire, including, of all people, Reps. Torricelli and Mrazek. All four had benefited from Connell's honoraria and/or campaign contributions. The group took lunch with Mobutu on his yacht, but he refused to allow them to visit Tshisekedi.

Ambassador Harrop later told me, "When I was critical of Mobutu, Connell tried to shut me up . . . [the legislators] really behaved in a numb way." Following their visit, Torricelli noted "subtle improvements" in human rights policies. More cautiously, Mrazek said he hoped for "some improvements."[52] Yet as time passed, not a single member among those Connell entertained or traveled with lifted a finger to protect the Mobutu regime from the rising tide of congressional disassociation.

These developments further underlined Mobutu's weakness as a congressional lobbyist. He had proved eminently successful in exploiting eight Democratic and Republican administrations' exaggerated fears of chaos and communism to seize power and consolidate personal rule. During the late 1960s, as declassified CIA documents reveal, Mobutu was even able to twice persuade the CIA to give him money to reimburse his army for his embezzlements, which he argued might be discovered and thereby threaten his pro-U.S. government.[53] But manipulating a democratic legislature was harder. It required different political talents and deep knowledge of the personal and power relations within the institution. From his abortive pro-Israel gambit to his collision with the Codel to his flirtations with Black Caucus leaders, Mobutu had demonstrated he lacked the right stuff.

CHAPTER 14

A SENSE OF AN ENDING

*I*n 1989, the House and Senate Foreign Affairs/
Relations and Appropriations committees agreed
for the first time on the same low number for military aid to
Zaire: $3 million. The administration had requested twice
that amount.

The outcome reflected Congress's continuing concerns
about political repression and military abuses. It was also
influenced by new evidence of massive corruption. In a general
conversation with Larry Saiers, a high USAID official who
was strongly committed to economic policy reforms in Africa,
I learned that the World Bank had postponed a meeting on
Zaire because it was unable to account for about $400 million
in missing foreign exchange receipts. In addition, Saiers let
me know that his own agency had suspended its private sector
project in Zaire because the government had not taken steps
to get its economic house in order.

I asked him if he was willing to say these things if questioned
at a public hearing. He was agreeable and Howard elicited that
testimony.[54] I am sure that if we had asked the State Department
about these matters rather than its semi-independent subsidiary
agency, we would not have gotten such clear answers.

Notwithstanding those revelations, when our subcommittee recommendation reached the full committee we heard that our very conservative Republican ranking member, Rep. Dan Burton (R-IN), was readying an amendment to fund the full $6 million request for military aid.

It happened that I had just received a September 1988 CIA analysis (since largely declassified) titled "Zaire: The Military Under Mobutu." Its lead paragraph read:

[Redacted] The Zairian military, after 23 years under President Mobutu, has become a weak, ineffective force that is incapable of defending the country's borders or of containing more than limited internal disorders. Many of the military's shortcomings stem from such fundamental problems as inadequate manpower, resources and military know-how [Redacted] Mobutu's strategy for ensuring military loyalty has been the major cause of military decline. His patronage network has fostered an epidemic of corruption, and his frequent manipulation of personnel and assignments has hampered effective leadership.[55]

I asked Howard to show the study to Burton. After he did, the latter withdrew his amendment.

Another Codel experience may have eased our way. Earlier in the year, on their way back to the United States from a visit to "freedom fighters" in Angola, Burton and three other House Republicans had stopped by President Mobutu's reconstructed "home village" of Gbadolite. A key Republican staffer later confided to me that the congressmen were "shocked" at what they observed: a rented Concord on the airport tarmac, palaces and villas under construction, a $3 million cathedral, giant gold urns, $400 bottles of French wine, and the presence of a notorious luncheon guest, Tongsun Park, a convicted congressional influence peddler from the 1970s "Koreagate" scandal. Perhaps that experience made it easier for Burton to back down.

In June 1989, President Mobutu attended a committee tea for the first time in six years. It was the only such occasion where I apparently did not take notes. Maybe I felt I'd heard it all before. I preserve a single memory from that session that made me think the president was further losing his touch. He lashed out at "Jewish diamond dealers in Antwerp" who were thwarting him. He seemed unaware that members of Congress around the table might smell a whiff of anti-Semitism.

June 1989: House Foreign Affairs Committee Tea with President Mobutu (with Leopard skin cap). Subcommittee Chairman Howard Wolpe to his right, Subcommittee member Mervyn Dymally two seats to the left.

By April 1990, the Cold War was ending and democracy movements were rising in Zaire, Africa, and worldwide. Sensing an opportunity, I urged Howard and Steve to ask to testify on Zaire before the key House Appropriations Subcommittee. The foreign aid authorizing committees were gradually losing power to their appropriations counterparts. (Congress did not bother to pass foreign assistance authorization bills for Fiscal Years 1983–85 and 1987–89.) We needed to adjust by upping our game with the Subcommittee on Foreign Operations.

Thus, Howard and Steve appeared at a public hearing and argued for the elimination of all military aid and a prohibition on economic aid through the government (rather than through private and voluntary organizations). Chairman David Obey (D-WI) assured them, "No bill that bears my name will have any money for that turkey [Mobutu]."[56] Toward the end of the year, his promise—essentially the position Steve and our committee had first advanced in 1979—was incorporated into law.

Around the same time, Howard informed our staff that he had decided, after ten fruitful years, to leave the chairmanship to assume a newly available chairmanship on a domestic policy subcommittee. (Under House rules, he was restricted to one subcommittee chairmanship at a time.) This was quite reasonable politically considering the interests of his Michigan constituents.

His successor would be none other than Rep. Dymally. The Californian chose to bring on an entirely new professional staff, as was his right. Not that I would have been willing to work for him, considering his transactional relationships with lobbyists regarding Zaire and, as press reports disclosed, Uganda, Angola and Southern African diamond interests.

I decided not to seek another position with Congress. After twelve years of working on multiple African issues, I was pretty burnt out by the intensity I had brought to my job, which inevitably carried over into my off-work hours. I recall my unfortunate compulsion, after a full day's work, to speed through the Foreign Broadcast Information Service's daily reports on African media stories during my long bus commutes home. My son Daniel still reminds me of how I would fall asleep, sitting up on the couch, while our family watched television together after dinner. Nancy and Daniel would wake me when my favorite program came on.

So, just as our long legislative drive on Zaire reached its culmination, my second engagement with Congo/Zaire came to an end.

~~~

POSTSCRIPT

S oon after I left Congress, a democratic movement
shook the Mobutu regime, forcing it to temporarily
cede some power to Tshisekedi and his popular UDPS. But
when Mobutu subsequently took back his democratic promises,
the U.S. stood aside. It did not use its considerable diplomatic
and economic weight—for example by marshaling Western
sanctions against his enormous, ill-gotten wealth—to pressure
the president to step down and allow free and fair elections.

The "Big Man," as the great writer V.S. Naipaul dubbed
him, was finally overthrown in 1997 by a rebel movement
organized and supported by neighboring Rwanda and Angola.
It was bolstered by other African nations that had long viewed
Mobutu's rule as a Western-imposed humiliation. Later, however, a regional war broke out among these former comrades
and their Congolese protégés, costing the lives of approximately
three and a half million people. Confronted with such an
enormous atrocity only a few years after they had done nothing
to stop the Rwandan genocide, the U.S. and other Western
governments backed creative South African diplomacy, which
achieved a peaceful, democratic settlement.

Regrettably, neither democracy nor total peace lasted very
long. The elected but increasingly authoritarian Joseph Kabila

regime began to be characterized as "Mobutu-lite." Dozens of armed groups took advantage of the Congo's weak, corrupt, abusive state and military to terrorize and economically exploit its Eastern provinces. Many of these groups received support from adjoining Rwanda and Uganda as well as segments of the Congo's armed forces. The U.S. government, still the most important Western actor, remained mired in its anachronistic Cold War reluctance to question a familiar "pro-Western" regime. This was the underlying meaning of policy makers' perpetual invocation of "stability" as a justification for its acquiescence.

Looking back thirty to forty years upon our congressional exertions, I think that by keeping the level of military and political support to the Mobutu regime much lower than administrations wished, we made it less likely that the U.S. would intervene, either politically or through CIA covert action, when the Mobutu regime was on the ropes. That would have only prolonged the crisis, raising the risks for U.S. relations. Furthermore, by showing, through both words and actions, Congress's concern for the democratic political opposition, we probably helped ensure that their successors, led by the UDPS's Étienne Tshisekedi, would continue to seek support in the U.S. and not become anti-American. Since 2019 the president of the Congo has been Tshisekedi's son, Félix.

In 2013, after two decades of working in various capacities on other foreign and domestic policies and programs, I again turned my attention toward Congo policy, this time as an unpaid outside advocate. Along with Tony Gambino, a former Peace Corps volunteer in Kisangani, congressional staff colleague, and USAID Congo Mission Director, I organized a coalition of nongovernmental organizations and experts to lobby the U.S. administration and Congress on behalf of democracy, human rights, anti-corruption measures, and an end to armed conflict. This continuing effort, along with studies I've published on contemporary U.S. policies toward Afghanistan, Libya, South Africa, Syria, and Ukraine, has shown me that many of the U.S. governmental dysfunctions we struggled with a few decades ago persist today.

~~~

ENDNOTES

1. Stephen R. Weissman, *A Culture of Deference: Congress's Failure of Leadership in Foreign Policy* (New York: Basic Books, 1995), p. 72.

2. The following six paragraphs are based on Stephen R. Weissman, *American Foreign Policy in the Congo 1960–1964* (Ithaca and London: Cornell University Press, 1974), supplemented by my subsequent articles based on declassified U.S. government files, "An Extraordinary Rendition," *Intelligence and National Security*, 25, 2 (April 2010), pp. 198–222; and "What Really Happened in Congo," *Foreign Affairs* (July/August 2014), pp. 14–24.

3. Ruth Kornfield-Gilman, "Relations Between Zairians and Europeans in the City of Kisangani A Symbolic Interactionist Approach," Unpublished Ph.D. thesis, University of Manchester, 1974, p. 68.

4. A survey of political opinion among Zairian university students during my time in the country showed that a majority of those who endorsed political ideologies (a plurality of those surveyed) chose "socialist" over "nationalist," with the latter characterized as supportive of the government. See Ntsomo Payanzo, "Education and Universities in a New

Nation: The Case of the Republic of Zaire," Unpublished Ph.D. thesis, Northwestern University, 1974, p. 245.

5. Galen Spencer Hull, *Crossing Cultures: Memoirs of a Travlin' Man* (Galen Spencer Hull, 2006), p. 300.

6. Kornfield-Gilman, "Relations Between Zairians," pp. 211–12.

7. From American Embassy Kinshasa to Secretary of State, Telegram 13, "ULC Situation," January 2, 1971, file EDU 9–3 THE CONGO, 1970–73 Subject-Numeric File, RG 59, General Records of the Department of State, U.S. National Archives.

8. From American Consulate Kisangani to Secretary of State, Aerogram A-15, "The University of Kisangani (Part I of II)," August 5, 1971, p.8, file EDU 9–3 THE CONGO, 1970–73 SNF, RG 59, USNA. Part II of this document, analyzing developments at the university flowing from the change of rectors, is missing from the National Archives.

9. Crawford Young and Thomas Turner, *The Rise and Decline of the Zairian State* (Madison: University of Wisconsin Press), 1981, p. 7; Crawford Young, *The Postcolonial State in Africa: Fifty Years of Independence, 1960–2010* (Madison: University of Wisconsin Press, 2012), pp. 137–38.

10. From American Embassy Kinshasa to Secretary of State, Telegram 1990, "Trouble at Kisangani University," March 27, 1971, file POL 23–8 THE CONGO, 1970–73 SNF, RG 59, USNA.

11. U.S. Department of State, *Foreign Relations of the United States*, 1969–76, *Southern Africa*, Vol. XXXVIII, Document 106, June 5, 1975.

12. Elise Forbes Pachter, "Our Man in Kinshasa: U.S. Relations with Mobutu 1970–83: Patron-Client Relations in the International Sphere," Unpublished Ph.D. dissertation, Johns Hopkins University, 1987, pp. 160–61.

13. From American Embassy Kinshasa to Secretary of State, Telegram 2246, "Steven Weisman," April 7, 1971, file POL 23–8 THE CONGO, 1970–73 SNF, RG 59, USNA.

14. Pedro A.G. Monaville, "Decolonizing the University: Postal Politics, the Student Movement and Global 1968 in the Congo," Unpublished Ph.D. dissertation, University of Michigan, 2013.

15. From American Embassy Kinshasa to Secretary of State, Telegram 2291, "Stephen Weissman," April 9, 1971, file POL 23–8 THE CONGO, 1970–73 SNF, RG 59, USNA.

16. House Committee on Foreign Affairs, *Foreign Assistance Legislation for Fiscal Years 1980–81:* Hearings and Markup before the Subcommittee on Africa. Part 6, 96th Cong., 1st sess., 1979, pp. xv–xvi, 351–441.

17. Senate Committee on Foreign Relations, To Markup S584 to Amend the Foreign Assistance Act of 1961 and the Arms Export Control Act, and for Other Purposes, May 3, 1979, pp. 93–97, typewritten transcript, NA.

18. Senate Committee on Foreign Relations and House Committee on Foreign Affairs, "Joint Conferees, H.R. 3173, International Security Assistance Act of 1979," July 31, 1979, pp. 20–33, typewritten transcript, NA.

19. House Committee on Foreign Affairs, *Foreign Assistance Legislation for Fiscal Year 1981:* Hearings and Markup before the Subcommittee on Africa, Part 7, 96th Cong.,

2nd sess.,1980, pp. xiii–xvi, 526–643, 652–56; House Committee on Foreign Affairs, *Foreign Assistance Legislation for Fiscal Year 1981 (Part 9)*, Full Committee Markup, 96th Cong. 2nd sess.,1980, pp.143–54.

20. Cord Meyer, "Zaire and our Iranian Syndrome," *Washington Star*, March 17, 1979.

21. Robert Moss, "Mole-Hunts in Washington," *London Daly Telegraph*, November 24, 1980.

22. Robert Moss, "Now the Reagan Transition," December 8, 1980.

23. Rowland Evans and Robert Novak, "Still Going After the CIA," *Washington Post*, February 2, 1981.

24. Letter to the Editor, "Completely out of Context," *Washington Post*, February 3, 1981.

25. See House Committee on Foreign Affairs, "Enforcement of the United States Arms Embargo Against South Africa," Hearing before the Subcommittee on Africa, March 30, 1982, 97th Cong. 2nd sess.

26. Pachter, "Our Man in Kinshasa," pp. 362–63.

27. *Ibid.*, p. 359.

28. David Brock, "The Prince Metternichs of Congress," *The American Spectator*, February 1990, p. 22; "Congo Din," Letter from Steve Weissman and reply by David Brock, in Correspondence, *The American Spectator*, April 1990. p. 9. Not to be quieted, Brock subsequently quoted a "ranking" State Department "Africanist" saying I was "more Stalinist than any member of the Soviet Politburo," in "The Rainbow Lobby Storms Congress," *The American Spectator*, November 1990, p. 24.

29. House Committee on Foreign Affairs, *Foreign Assistance Legislation for Fiscal Year 1982) (Part 8),* Hearings and Markup before the Subcommittee on Africa, 1981, pp. 123, xiv–xvi.

30. Senate Committee on Foreign Relations and House Committee on Foreign Affairs, Joint Conferees, S 1196, International Security and Development Assistance Act of 1981, December 14, 1981, typewritten transcript (author's copy).

31. House Committee on Foreign Affairs, *Political and Economic Situation in Zaire – Fall 1981,* Hearing before the Subcommittee on Africa, November 10, 1981, 97th Cong. 1st sess.

32. A.Z.A.P., "Reactions zairoises aux accusations de Nguza," Septembre 17, 1981.

33. House Committee on Foreign Affairs, "*Foreign Assistance Legislation for Fiscal Year 1983 (Part 7),* Hearings and Markup before the Subcommittee on Africa, 97th Cong. 2nd sess., pp. 120–173, xiii–xiv.

34. House Committee on Foreign Affairs, *Foreign Assistance Legislation for Fiscal Year 1983 (Part 8),* Full Committee Markup, 1982, 97th Cong. 2nd sess., pp. 186–88.

35. Paris, *Agence France-Presse* (Foreign Broadcast Information Service Translation), May 13, 1982. For reference to Zaire's two-year departure from the worldwide diamond marketing cartel controlled by De Beers, see "Can Mobutu Persuade the West to Bail Out Zaire?" *Business Week,* October 12, 1983.

36. In August 1981, Zaire replaced its previous lobbyists with the Hampton-Windsor Corporation, headed by a former official of the B'nai B'rith Anti-Defamation League, a leading American Jewish organization. The company was to receive $1.2 million for two years. See U.S. Department of Justice, Foreign Agents Registration Statement, Hampton-Windsor Corporation, August 17, 1981.

37. Senate Committee on Foreign Relations, *Zaire: A Staff Report to the Committee on Foreign Relations United States Senate*, July 1982, 97th Cong. 2nd sess.

38. House Committee on Foreign Affairs, *Foreign Assistance Legislation for Fiscal Years 1984–85 (Part 9)*, Markup, 1983, 98th Cong. 1st sess., pp. 387–95.

39. Weissman, *A Culture of Deference*, pp. 91–92.

40. House Committee on Foreign Affairs, *Foreign Assistance Legislation for Fiscal Years 1986–87 (Part 8)*, Markup 1985, 99th Cong. 1st sess., p. 192. See also Weissman, *A Culture of Deference*, p. 91.

41. The official report of the Codel to Zaire is found in House Committee on Foreign Affairs, *The Impact of U.S. Foreign Policy on Seven African Countries*, Report of a Congressional Study Mission to Ethiopia, Zaire, Zimbabwe, Ivory Coast, Algeria and Morocco, August 6–25, 1983, and a Staff Study to Tunisia, August 24–27, 1983, March 9, 1984, pp. 1–2, 27–36, 61–63.

42. American Embassy, Algiers (3501) to Secretary of State, August 21, 1983, "Codel Wolpe's Comments." (Declassified)

43. House Committee on Foreign Affairs, *Foreign Assistance Legislation for Fiscal Year 1985 (Part 7)*, Markup before the Subcommittee on Africa, 1984, 98th Cong., 2nd sess., p. 4.

44. Part of the following discussion of the Rainbow Lobby is based on my factual research for Weissman, *A Culture of Deference*, pp. 96–99.

45. On the Leland/Connell financial relationship, see *Ibid.,* pp. 78–79.

46. *Ibid.,* pp. 79, 99–100.

47. Part of the following four paragraphs is based on my factual research for *Ibid.,* pp. 93–96.

48. House Committee on Foreign Affairs, *Foreign Assistance Legislation for Fiscal Years 1984–85, p. 394.*

49. Weissman, *A Culture of Deference*, p. 95.

50. *Ibid.,* pp. 95–96.

51. House Committee on Foreign Affairs, *Foreign Assistance Legislation for Fiscal Years 1990–91 (Part 6)*, Hearings and Markup before the Subcommittee on Africa, 1989, 101st Cong. 1st sess., pps. 117, 335–74.

52. Weissman, *A Culture of Deference*, pp. 78–9, 100–101.

53. Weissman, "What Really Happened in Congo," *Foreign Affairs* (July/August 2014), p. 21.

54. *Foreign Assistance Legislation for Fiscal Years 1990–91*, p. 104.

55. Central Intelligence Agency, Directorate of Intelligence, "Zaire: The Military Under Mobutu," December 1988. (Declassified)

56. Clifford Krauss, "House Democrats Challenge Bush by Seeking to Reduce Aid to Zaire," *New York Times*, April 11, 1990.

ACKNOWLEDGMENTS

I wish to thank the following colleagues, friends, and family for their useful comments on a shorter draft of Part I that I circulated several years ago: Lynn Adams, Daniel Weissman, Thomas Turner, Ruth Kornfield-Gilman and the late Charles Gilman, Mary and Alistair Weir, Georges Nzongola, Harvey Graff, René Lemarchand, Herbert Weiss, Bruce Kuklick, Adam Hochschild, Stuart Reid and the late Crawford Young. Here, I owe a particular debt to Cissi Falligant, whose editorial expertise contributed to a stronger, more reader-centered narrative.

Accompanying me during my congressional journey throughout Africa were my wonderful bosses, the late House Subcommittee on Africa Chairmen, Stephen Solarz and Howard Wolpe, and my supportive subcommittee staff colleagues: Johnnie Carson, David Frank, Sarah Lisenby, Priscilla Newman, Mickey Harmon, the late Anne Forrester, Salih Booker, Stephen Morrison, Adwoa Dunn-Mouton, and Mark Quarterman. Nothing would have been possible for us on the Congo and other African issues without them.

A special note of appreciation to Adam Hochschild and Stuart Reid, whose valuable comments on my book proposal helped me better understand the import of what I have written.

A NOTE ABOUT
THE AUTHOR

Stephen R. Weissman is the author of *American Foreign Policy in the Congo 1960–1964* (Cornell University Press, 1974) and *A Culture of Deference: Congress's Failure of Leadership in Foreign Policy* (Basic Books, 1995, 1996). Other writings relevant to this book include, "The Cold War's Cold Cases: What Really Happened in Congo," *Foreign Affairs* (July–August 2014) and "Why did Washington Let a Stolen Election in the Congo Stand?" *Foreign Policy*, April 28, 2021.

A political scientist, Weissman has taught and researched at Fordham University, New Jersey City University, Stanford University, University of Texas at Dallas, and Howard University. He has published widely on American foreign policy in various regions of the the world and on American campaign finance issues.